CELEBRATE
YOUR SELF

by the author

CELEBRATE YOUR SELF
YOUR CHILD'S SELF-ESTEEM
EMBRACING LIFE

CELEBRATE YOUR SELF

ENHANCING YOUR SELF-ESTEEM

by

Dorothy Corkille Briggs

DOUBLEDAY & COMPANY, INC. · GARDEN CITY, NEW YORK

From "Little Gidding" in *Four Quartets*, copyright, 1943 by T. S. Eliot; renewed, © 1971, by Esme Valerie Eliot. Reprinted by permission of Harcourt Brace Jovanovich, Inc. and Faber and Faber Ltd.

Library of Congress Cataloging-in-Publication Data

Briggs, Dorothy Corkille.
    Celebrate your self.

    1. Self-respect.   2. Transactional analysis.
I. Title.
BF575.S414B75   1986   158'.1   85–29260
ISBN 0–385–13105–4

Dedicated to
your *decision* to let go of your negative conditioning
and
your *choice* to become one with the You that truly is.

We shall not cease from exploration
And the end of all our exploring
Will be to arrive where we started
And know the place for the first time.

T. S. ELIOT

This offering is made with appreciation and love and hope.

I *appreciate* the priceless gifts of caring, understanding support, sharing and affirmation from my dear family, friends and the many people whose lives have touched mine. Each has given in his or her own unique way.

I *love* the gift of Life. I love the opportunity to touch the Life in others. I love the fact that each of us has the choice to grow and make our possibilities come true.

I *hope* this book provides the awareness, inspiration and courage to use its suggested tools. Then you will be free to celebrate your Self—the basis for celebrating others.

Special thanks to Jim, Jan Olsen and Susie Veroda for their perceptive reactions to this manuscript; to Jan for her careful typing; to Jim for this book's title.

Dorothy Corkille Briggs

Rancho Palos Verdes
California

If you are not for you
Who will be?
If you are only for you
What's the purpose?
If not now, when?

HILLEL

CONTENTS

CELEBRATE
YOUR SELF

PART I
THE PRISON

· ONE ·

WHAT'S HERE FOR YOU

In quiet moments do you sometimes feel you are in a mute search for something that's missing? If so, you are not alone.

A great hunger lies across the land. Regardless of age, sex or race, a vague dis-ease—if not outright desperation—pervades. A lot of active seeking with little permanent finding.

In our quest most of us chase the rainbows of success, power, prestige or the approval of others. Surely, we reason, what's just beyond will bring peace and a sense of purpose. But once we have what we thought would do the trick, we find the treasure has eluded us.

Regardless of outer pluses too many feel lonely and unloved. Yet we keep on trying to get something from "out there" to still the inner unrest. And we cannot pinpoint what's amiss.

We may try encounter groups, weekend marathons and pop psych offerings hoping to find "it." Chemicals, trips or affairs. A magic pill for instant ease. The last place we seem to look is within.

As social beings our lasting satisfactions and meanings are in relationships. We each need to love and be loved, to stroke and be stroked—not only physically but psychologically. How much we can love or let in love is based on how you and I *relate*. Successfully or unsuccessfully.

Long before you can improve your relationships with others, however, you first need to improve your relationship to yourself. For,

> **You will do unto others**
> **as you do unto yourself.**

If you drive yourself incessantly, you may be sure you'll push others relentlessly. If you constantly find fault with yourself, you will look for what's wrong in "them." We are told to "Love others *as* ourselves." Most of us do precisely that. We do not affirm ourselves and we bombard others with the same treatment. If you do not value your own Being you cannot cherish others. Improving your relationship to yourself is where the action is. The treasure you seek lies within.

Yes, each of us can write our own ticket to inner serenity. Yet few of us are aware that the key lies in ongoing Self affirmation. In short,

> **The inwardly content**
> **are able to handle love.**

And that calls, first and foremost, for joy of Self. *It is the by-product of wholehearted Self celebration that brings inner peace.*

Because self-worth is contagious, you will almost automatically nurture those around you once your self-esteem is high. For,

> **How you feel about yourself**
> **directly affects**
> **how you live life,**
> **how you relate to others.**

Self-love vs. conceit

We commonly think of self-love as selfishness or conceit. We see it as bragging, thinking only of ourselves and putting ourselves above others.

Yet the person who is out to grab everything for himself actually feels deprived. He feels unlucky and needs to hoard to erase his inner misfortune. He brags and cockwalks in a sad attempt to make himself feel better.

The compliment he receives, however, seems beside the point an hour later because he does not say "Yes" to his own Being. The outer plus does not stick; the accumulations do not fill the inner void.

If you live with quiet, deep gladness about your person, you don't need outer trappings or constant strokes to reassure yourself that you are OK. Yet because you affirm your worth and value, you let in outer affirmation when it comes.

With a full "cupboard" you don't need to knock others down to get. You are in a far better position to share, reach out, give and receive. Remember,

**Conceit only masks
lack of true self-love.**

Where the answer lies

The alternative to inner unrest and unhappiness, the alternative to passing this on to the next generation then is to increase your own sense of self-worth . . . to free the Real You. It is difficult, if not impossible, to experience ongoing inner quiet and purpose without a solid belief in your True Self.

You cannot always change the outer or others to your liking. But you can change the inner and your reaction to what happens.

Clear about wanting to increase our self-esteem, many of us are quite unclear as to how to do it. What we search for are specifics. This book provides them. It takes you where you are today and lays out the road map for how to get where you want to go. It gives you a handle on what's wrong while showing you how to make it right. And when you feel right with yourself, you feel right with the world.

You probably wouldn't have picked up this book unless some force within was whispering, "My life can be more rewarding." Listen to that urge. An inner push to fulfill the promise of your birth exists within you. Regardless of your past you can wriggle free of a limiting self-image and sail forth to inner gladness, a life that tastes sweet.

Certainly some of you need a professional assist for the trip. And no book replaces the corrective emotional experience that an affirming person gives. But by following the guidelines set forth here many have moved from self-put-downs and loser choices to Self celebration and the winner's circle. These ideas are people-tested.

Tools for the trip

To increase your self-worth the first step is to be *aware* of the past programming you used to build your present "Me" package. I'll show you how this process took place.

Then I'll give you the specific tools for redesigning your identity so that you celebrate your Self with quiet gladness.

With this awareness and a set of proven tools available for your use, the real issue will be: *how motivated are you to set yourself free?* If you are tired of the games or apathy or pain, this discontent is your friend. There is nothing like being fed up to push you into trying the new.

Awareness and motivation flourish with your willingness to risk total self-honesty. Your willingness to risk challenging old assumptions and beliefs. Your willingness to change.

Such risk-taking calls for courage. It calls for an adventuresome spirit. It calls for an inner decision to move out and try the new.

You won't need will power but rather commitment. And if commitment comes hard we'll look at who and what holds you back.

Above all,

Awareness, courage and decision
need to be coupled
with action.

Recipes in books don't bake cookies. You do—through action. Blueprints on paper don't build bridges. People hard at work do. Here are the tools you need. But only you can decide to use them, to practice them daily.

The great temptation

As you read, it will be almost irresistibly tempting to apply the ideas to your friends, loved ones, neighbors all around. In fact, you might like to read this book the first time giving yourself the privilege of applying everything to others. That's easy and kind of fun.

Then make an agreement with yourself to reread and insist that you apply each concept only to yourself. For if you truly want to increase your self-worth, you will need to

Take your eyes
off the other
and look to yourself.

Even with such a totally dedicated self-promise, we all have a tendency to be Professional Wrigglers. "This apply to me? Certainly not!" Most of us have a vested interest in wriggling off the hook. But each time we do, we hold back growth. And that means cheating ourselves of the very thing we want and need—wholeness.

Background ideas

The simple model of Parent-Adult-Child from Transactional Analysis (TA) gives an easy framework to better understand how you got where you are today. It helps you see how and why you stay "stuck" through your self-talk.

We'll use this model as a backdrop against which to weave the significant contributions from the various schools of psychological thought (analytic, gestalt, rational-emotive, non-directive, reality, primal, bioenergetics, transactional, psychocybernetics, meditational and transpersonal).

I don't believe any single approach can claim an exclusive for how to become whole and inwardly free. But by pulling together the major insights into the human condition, a blueprint for increasing your own self-esteem emerges. By following these guidelines you can say "Yes" to your Being.*

To understand the specifics for freeing the Real You, you will need only the simple overview of TA covered in Chapter Three. Should you already be familiar with its more elaborate details, you may be tempted to skip this chapter. I invite you to resist the temptation. Skim, maybe, but not skip.

The key to joyful living lies squarely in challenging who you think you are. Before jumping into your personality makeup, let's look briefly at your most important characteristic—your sense of identity. For your Belief System about You is the touchstone to how you experience life.

* The ideas here may be considerably buttressed by reading my earlier book, *Your Child's Self-Esteem*. (Available from Doubleday in hardcover and Dolphin in paperback.) Although that book was written for parents and teachers, it is basically concerned with the nature and needs—the tapestry —of the human fabric. In reading it you may find out a great deal about your "Me" that will increase your ability to put the ideas here into practice.

· TWO ·

YOUR BELIEF SYSTEM ABOUT YOU

Your identity

Who are you?

Where are you headed?

Does it make a difference that you exist?

Increasingly these questions have received attention. And they need to be looked at. Your particular answers affect whether you experience gladness, the blahs or desperation. These crucial questions surface for each of us from time to time. No one escapes them.

How do *you* answer, "Who are you?"

With your name? It's important to you but literally it is a group of *sounds* to identify you. If you had another name would you necessarily be a different Being? You're a woman, a man, a teen? You tell me about your *sexual characteristics* and *age*. Surely they form part of your identity but such does not let me know You.

You're a salesperson, a secretary, a student? A wife, husband, parent, friend? These describe some of your *activities* and *relationships*, of course. But knowing about them or your various *physical features* leaves me in the dark about who *You* are. Who's the You inside your particular package? And apart from what you do?

These popular ways of identifying yourself to others skirt the real issue. Faced with this, you may say, "I guess I don't know who *I* am."

Knowing your values gives me a feel for where you are anchored, what you hold fast to. It lets me into your head. But it still does not give me direct human contact with the Real You.

I am closest to knowing the Real You when you put me in touch with the dynamic, unique Essence that is always in process—in the ebb and flow of unfolding as only your particularness can. Then you let me into your center. To know the Real You I need to make contact with your Essential Being—the You unlike any other.

If you tell me that deep down you are a person of little worth, you share your self-image. Your dim self-picture says who you *think* you are but actually only describes the *kinds of relationships* you've had with important life persons.

Your self-image—who you think you are—is literally a package *you put together* from how others have seen and treated you and from your conclusions as you compared yourself to others. Your sense of identity is the end result of the interaction between your uniqueness and how others have reacted to it. It is the package you call "Me." But it does not tell me about your Real Self. For most of us, "Know thyself" means "Know what important others thought of you."

It is never who *You* are that hangs you up, but rather who you *think* you are. Be aware that

**Your self-image is learned;
your Real Self is a given.**

To discover your Real Self it is important to separate the Real You from your self-image. This idea can be seen in the diagram on the following page. Lining up your self-picture to fit the Real You is a task of utmost importance. There is probably no more exciting journey than that of Real Self discovery. Once your Self Belief System is accurate you are free of the trap of low self-esteem. You are free to be the Real You.

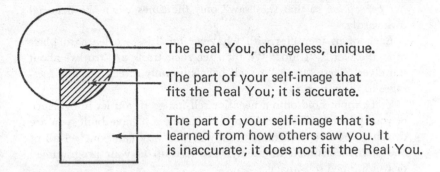

The Real You, changeless, unique.

The part of your self-image that fits the Real You; it is accurate.

The part of your self-image that is learned from how others saw you. It is inaccurate; it does not fit the Real You.

Past teachings limit

Primitive people built homes from the materials available in their surroundings—blocks of ice, animal skins, adobe, logs. They had no other choice at the time.

Just so, as a child you built your House of Self—your sense of identity—from what was available. *Your construction materials were the reactions of significant others toward you.* As we've mentioned, how those others saw you became how you saw yourself. In childhood you had no other choice.

If you were exposed to large doses of put-downs and belittlers, your set of Self beliefs is correspondingly dim. If you grew up in a basically positive person-to-person psychological climate your "Me" package feels good to live in.

The conclusions you came to about yourself formed your answers to "Who am I?" Your self-image is simply a Belief System you have constructed about yourself.

These past learnings jell into self-statements which may or may not be accurate. But once formed, *you see them as accurate regardless of the facts.*

Stella, for instance, was repeatedly told as a child that she was clumsy. Because she bought that label, she ignored or denied any evidence of her gracefulness. Graceful and clumsy don't mix; they are inconsistent with one another. Like all of us, Stella sought to build a consistent self-picture. To hold onto her "clumsy" self-statement, she erased any inputs to the contrary as fast as they came in.

A past teaching limited the accuracy of her self-image. It *froze her perception* so that she "saw" only the times when she behaved awkwardly.

Each of us identifies with whatever qualities we learn to place after the words "I am." We then see such traits as "truths" about ourselves. These "truths" or self-beliefs literally screen out any messages to the contrary.

You cannot hold onto a negative self-image if you let in evidence of your positives. Then to keep the identity you have built, you are driven to behave accordingly. Only in this way can you feel all of one piece—consistent internally. You live up to your programmed or conditioned self-image.

Your behavior will match your picture of yourself.

Here's a simple physical exercise that clearly illustrates how past teachings limit your behavior.

Stand with your feet about one foot apart. Raise your arms up from your sides to shoulder height. Now drop your right hand to the outside of your right thigh and see how far you can slide it down the outside of your right leg toward your right ankle. Stop when the movement becomes a strain. Return to standing position. Do this now before you read further.

How far down were you able to go? Most people bend over to their right side, keep their knees straight and are unable to touch their ankle. Is this what you did?

Now stand with your arms out at shoulder level on either side of your body. Let your right hand follow your right thigh toward your right ankle. But this time *bend your knees* as you go down to your right ankle. Return to standing position. Do this now. With this set of instructions you were undoubtedly able to reach your ankle comfortably.

Why didn't you do this with the first set of instructions? You were simply told that first time to move your right hand down your right thigh to see how close you could come to your right ankle. Nothing was said about *not* bending your knees in the first set of instructions.

The limiting idea that probably kept you from bending your

knees was your past experience with calisthenics or physical education classes. Teachers told you that the "correct" way to touch your ankles was to keep your knees straight. So, as you followed the first instructions just now, reaching your right ankle by bending your knees was prevented by a past teaching: "Keep your knees straight." You made an *automatic assumption based on past exposures* that the choice of knee bending was unopen to you.

You doubt that without such past teachings you would have handled the first set of instructions differently? Imagine yourself as a three-year-old (uncontaminated by any prior instructions or modeling about the "proper" way to get your hand to your ankle). As a three-year-old wouldn't you simply bend your knees automatically with the first set of instructions? If you doubt this, try it out on any unprogrammed toddler. This exercise illustrates how

Past teachings
can limit your options.

In just the same way old teachings from your past hang like an invisible cloud to limit your picture of yourself. If your self-worth is low or shaky, you are still believing things about yourself that are untrue . . . negative ideas programmed into you about who You are. And, to repeat, you act accordingly.

There was a prisoner who spent years in his little cell totally unaware that his door was unlocked. At any point he could have walked out. But because he *assumed* there was an automatic lock on the door, he remained trapped. His false belief limited his behavior.

Whether this story is true or not is beside the point. Once you are aware that you are not locked into your present prison of discontent or self-doubt, whole sets of new choices open up. New ways to see yourself, new ways to relate, new ways to behave.

These choices have been there all along. The problem has been you did not know you had other options. You have been like the person programmed about the "proper" way to get a hand down to the ankle, like the unaware prisoner who made a false assumption.

Lack of awareness, of course, *is the same as having no choice.* As you become aware of the dynamics we'll discuss you can choose to stay with your inner dis-ease or you can choose to walk clear of it. I'm banking on your walking free.

At some point we all need to ask, "Which do I want for myself— prison or freedom?"

The door to your personal freedom is unlocked. You were born for joy. But only you can claim your rightful inheritance. The choice is yours no matter what your age. You and you alone in the final analysis design your world. If you vote for inner freedom, little can hold you back.

Levels of self-esteem

Although how you feel about yourself varies at different times, today you operate by and large from one of three levels of self-worth. You are either a self-hater, self-doubter or self-affirmer.

Low self-esteemers are convinced of their inferiority and feel unlovable. They put unreasonably high demands on themselves and are strongly self-critical. They are fearful of social situations and are easily discouraged. Expecting to fail, they have a "why try" attitude. They tend to be on the sidelines of life, isolated loners. They tend to listen rather than participate and are highly sensitive to criticism. They are preoccupied with inner problems. Much of their creativity is channeled into highly creative ways to fail.

Middle self-esteemers, the self-doubters, are more optimistic and expressive and can take some criticism. They tend to be conformists and compliant because they are quite dependent on social acceptance. This means they are not venturesome; they have to check out the safety factor first. They seek outside recognition and approval to erase self-doubt. Unsureness is the key. People-pleasing at all costs often results. If you live with driving ambition, are a "climber," are never satisfied, continually play a role to please others, you probably fit this category.

High self-esteemers, the self-validators, basically feel Self confident. This makes them eager to get involved wholeheartedly, to express themselves. It gives them courage to stand up for their convictions. They are not isolated nor loners. They can take criticism, tolerate frustration and are not threatened by failure. They tend to be physically healthy, enjoy life and have a positive outlook. They are not critical of themselves although they are realistically aware of both their strengths and shortcomings.

If the loser or doubter characteristics describe you, remember, you can choose to change your Self Belief System. And it is imperative that you do. For each low self-esteemer has one choice. Either increase self-worth or it decreases with age. Why?

Negative self-statements mean that only evidence fitting a dim self-view is let in. Therefore, your collection against yourself piles up with each passing year. And your self-worth sinks lower and lower. In short, untreated neurosis is progressive.

This downward spiral does not need to happen if you decide to challenge past teachings.

Self-image check

Here is a simple exercise to give a direct, personal check on your degree of self-esteem.

Read these instructions; then close your eyes and follow them.

Sit in a comfortable position, legs and arms uncrossed. Imagine an empty chair facing you. Picture a person who is very special and dear to you sitting on this chair. There may be many such people in your life, but choose only one. It can be any person, alive or dead.

Imagine that person as vividly as you can. See him or her in clear detail: features, clothes, coloring, characteristics. Avoid continuing the exercise until you have this person very sharply in focus. Begin to share with this person all the caring tenderness you feel for him or her. Spell out your loving feelings in such detail that the other would not have the slightest doubt as to your feelings. Take as much time as you need to get the message across.

Once you have told the other all the love feelings in your heart, tenderly reach out and give that person a hug, a kiss, or do whatever would be natural for you to do in the situation. Then, bid him or her a gentle goodbye for the time being and open your eyes.

Close your eyes now and proceed with this exercise.

Now that you have finished, check how you feel. If you are doing this exercise with others, take time to share whom you placed on the chair and how it really felt to open up and express your caring to your loved other.

The second half of this exercise again involves closing your eyes after you've read the instructions. Once again, be sure you are sitting in a comfortable, open position. Imagine that you are suddenly twins. (If you are a twin, imagine that you have a new twin who is part of your You.) Place this other You on the imaginary chair. Take time to see each of your features clearly; note your coloring, clothes and particular characteristics.

Once you have yourself on the chair in vivid detail, share with your Self how deeply you care for this You. Leave no detail out in expressing your tender joy for all that this Self means to you. Spend as much time in your Self dialogue as you did with the loved other. Then reach out, gently embrace this imaginary You and fantasize that the You-on-the-chair melts into the You-who-is-talking. Then slowly open your eyes. Now do the exercise.

If you are doing this with others, share what you experienced when you placed your Self in the love chair.

How was the dialogue between you and the loved other different from the one between you and You?

Some of you found you could share loving thoughts with the other but none at all with your You. Or you may have found that as soon as you shared a little bit of love talk with You, you began to think of all your shortcomings. Some of you may have discovered that your Self dialogue involved only a trickle of caring or a watered-down version—nothing very deep. Some of you found you could speak as wholeheartedly of your affection to You as to your loved other.

Only if you experienced the last situation do you have genuinely high self-esteem, a heartfelt appreciation for the wonder of You. Don't despair if you could not joyously affirm yourself. It only means you need to work on your Self Belief System. And that's what this book is all about.

Winners and losers

Throughout the past and in most places today winning means being on top. You have or are more of something than others. Traditionally this has meant you have more knowledge, money, power, status, fame, possessions, attractiveness, achievements or success.

"She's a winner," implies she's ahead of others as judged by some external. Conversely, "loser" is used for those who haven't made it in one or more of these categories.

Yet looking closely at those who have won by such standards, we don't necessarily find such people living with inner peace. How often we say, "He has everything that should make him happy, but he isn't." We see for ourselves that the outer does not guarantee happiness. Yet in our own personal quest we scramble after these time-honored tangibles. And we often feel threatened by others who have them.

Recently the great wave of humanism has shown us that

The real winners
are those who are fully
their human uniqueness.

The real losers are those who are not free to be what they were born to be—themselves. Disowning blocks of the Self they were meant to be, they have disconnected from the core of their Being. They might win by all exterior standards but they remain losers in life and love. They have forsaken the joy and power of being true to themselves.

Throughout this book when I talk about winners or winning, I refer to the person who is whole and inwardly free. When I talk about losers or losing I mean the person who is a slave to the Big Lie—the belief "I am not lovable and special." The loser bases his or her life on Not-OKness.

Suggestion for proceeding

My hope is that you will use this book as a workbook. You may want to read it through once to get the over-all picture. But if this is all you do, you cheat yourself. •

I suggest you read Chapters One through Four. Then starting with Chapter Five read only one chapter at a time. Avoid going to the next chapter until you have thoroughly digested the one completed. This will mean diligently doing the exercises and following the suggestions.

Only after you have done the homework and assimilated the material in Chapter Five will you take on Chapter Six. You will be allowing yourself to try out and make each new step part of your way of being with You before biting off another assignment.

Growth proceeds in little steps. And you do yourself an injustice by asking yourself to try everything at once. It may be a temptation to do so. Hopefully you'll choose to resist it. Top off your reading with Chapter Fourteen.

Let's look now at how you got to where you are today.

· THREE ·

HOW YOU GOT WHERE YOU ARE TODAY

Your mind as a tape recorder

To compare your mind to a tape recorder is to vastly underrate its enormous complexity. But for our purposes let's think of part of it as a multi-decked one. Each of us flips from one tape to another depending on the situation. Then we think, speak or act off that particular tape.

For example, imagine scolding your misbehaving ten-year-old Freddy with your "If I've told you once I've told you a hundred times" lecture. In the midst of it the phone rings. You move to answer it with a threatening, "Don't go away, young man, because I haven't finished with you yet."

Picking up the receiver you calmly and objectively say, "He-el-lo." (Pause) "Oh, Martha, I'll get that report to you tonight after dinner. Yes, I'll be at Thursday's meeting and . . ."

Just as you're speaking in this tone to Martha your husband comes home. Imagine that he asks very little except to please have dinner on the table at night as he eats no lunch and comes home ravenous. You feel this is little enough to ask. But it's been one of those days. Not only is dinner unprepared, you haven't even thought about what to serve.

You quickly end your phone visit, turn to your husband with a little-girl, placating tone and say, "Oh, honey, I am so sorry. Really, it's been one interruption after another. The repairman has been in the sink all afternoon" . . . and so on.

Here in rapid succession you flip from an angry scolder, to a casual conversationalist, to a pleading child. Have you ever wondered how you can switch "personalities" so rapidly? It's almost like having different people inside you depending on the situation.

Which tape is on?

This phenomenon happens to all of us. It only means that we can speak from any one of our inner "tapes."

The first step in self-awareness is to recognize that these tapes exist.

The next is to tune in to which one is on. In the example above when you talked to Freddy, you were in your Critical Parent tape; you switched to your Adult in speaking to Martha and then to your Not-OK Child Voice as you spoke to your husband.

Most of us think when we say "I" that we refer to a single entity, our inner Self. *But actually there are several "I's" in you.* Each one can be sent to the center of your stage and become the speaker.

Behind your tapes is the Real You. Getting in touch with your Essential Being makes constructive tape choices far more likely.

The repertoire of parts available to you can be seen in the diagram on the following page.

It's as if each of these parts is a separate entity within you. Altogether they represent your personal cast of characters.

Becoming aware of which "I" you give the power of center stage to is extremely important. A central question to ask yourself all along this trip is

Which "I" is
thinking, talking or acting?

Learning to identify your "I's" makes it easier to discover "who-in-you" is running your life. And to change the drama if you don't like the scene. The ideas here will show your Adult how to decrease the power you may have given to your Critical Parent and Not-OK

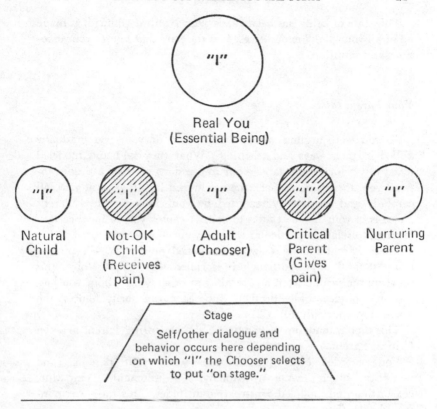

Child so they no longer control your life. It will then be up to your Adult to choose to put these ideas into practice.

Let's see how each of these parts came into being before we consider how to channel them to work for your best interest.

Your Natural Child

When you were born you were totally open to all inner and outer experiences including the body language of others. And you freely expressed your reactions toward these experiences. Spontaneity, playfulness, intuitiveness, creativity and impulsiveness—all of these were a part of what you came into the world with. You had an inner body wisdom that you listened to and responded with.

This state of being has been called your Natural Child; it is made up of all your "felt" experiences. It is the part that houses your emotions and intuition.

Your Parent tape

As you were around whoever took care of you, you gradually pulled in their ways and teachings. What they said and modeled jelled into your Parent tape. Your impressions of their attitudes toward you, themselves, others, the world and life in general were all carefully and assiduously recorded by you. This phantom Parent Voice is in your head. It talks to you. It causes you to have certain feelings, to relate in particular ways to yourself and others.

These Parent messages—what happened outside you—represent your "taught" tape. Although it is called the Parent Voice, this programming came from any significant other with whom you had ongoing contact (older brothers and sisters, authority figures, the media and your culture).

This tape is made up of two parts: the Nurturing Parent and the Critical Parent.

You recorded Nurturing messages when your parents (and significant others) were trustworthy, non-judgmental, empathic, comforting and modeled constructive attitudes. This tape was reinforced each time

1. they were appreciative, supportive and kept their requests in line with what you could comfortably handle at the time;
2. they showed that you counted even when your behavior needed changing; they separated your personal worth from your acts;
3. they saw what was right and positive about you; basically they were "for" you;
4. they believed in and increasingly supported your own power to control yourself;
5. they met your physical and psychological needs with friendly co-operation and without unreasonable delays.

Since no parent is nurturing 100 per cent of the time, certain of their ways formed your Critical Parent tape. It was programmed into being each time they judged, punished, scolded, spanked, deprived, blamed and found fault. It was enlarged each time

1. they overcontrolled;
2. their demands were impossible for you to meet;
3. they imposed overly strict "should's," "ought's," "must's," "have to's," "can'ts";
4. they focused on what was wrong and missing;
5. they taught, "You are what you do"; your personal worth went down the drain with each misstep;
6. they were basically "against" you in that they had little faith in you;
7. they taught you to look to *others* to control you;
8. they taught you to disregard your intuitiveness and some or all of your feelings.

Sometimes you may have felt rejected, put down or uncared for when that wasn't the case. As a small child you may have had to wait for others to come to your aid when you called or reached out. Your folks may not have heard you, may have been busy with something else, may have been sick or under too many personal pressures to be able to respond at that moment. They may have snapped or ignored only because they were tired. Regardless of how logical their behavior may have been to an adult, you as a young child may have recorded an "I don't count" message.

So your Critical Parent tape was enlarged by anything that you, as an unknowing child, felt as a discount regardless of its reasonableness.

By the time you learned to talk you started to mimic the party line of those around you. Does it seem strange to think of a two-year-old as having a Parent tape?

One father shared that his home had been child-proofed as much as possible. However, there was no way to fence off the books on the hall shelves. He and his wife taught their two that touching the books was a "no-no." One day as the father came into the hall he saw his son pull a book off the shelf, drop it on the floor and then spank his own hand, saying, "*Bad* Bobby." He pulled off another book, dropped it, slapped his hand again and scolded, "Shame, Bobby." Down the line of books he went.

Each time he pulled a book off he was on his Natural Child tape, doing what he wanted to do on impulse. Then he immediately flipped to his Critical Parent and scolded his Inner Child just as his parents had. Children develop Parent tapes very early. You have only to listen to toddlers to capture the flavor of their taping.

Two threes are playing together.

"Let's play house. You be baby. I be momma."

"OK."

"Get to bed, baby, or I swat ya." (Critical Parent Voice)

On the other hand that last sentence might have been,

"It's nite-nite-time, baby. Lemme sing loolaby to ya." (Nurturing Parent tape)

The Critical Voice then features put-downs and shrivelers. The Nurturing tape is made of self-esteem builders.

Your Not-OK Child tape

Once the Critical Parent tape is programmed something happens to the Natural Child. It now divides. The Natural Child remains but is repressed by a new tape called the Not-OK Child.

This new part of you comes into being and feeds on put-down messages. Because it *believes* the Critical Voice, your Not-OK Child feels helpless, picked on, rejected, guilty, lonely, overlooked, rebellious, bad, deprived or unloved. This tape is made up of all your negative feelings—your inner responses as a small, dependent, inept child.

Critical Parent messages have a far greater impact on the highly sensitive child than on the less sensitive one. A mildly cross tone may cause a marked startle in one and not even be noticed by another. *The impact of what goes on outside the child is always coupled with his or her particular genetic makeup.* Some of you were genetically more susceptible to such influences than others.

Your parents may not have been critical of you at all. They may have controlled by laying a continual "good boy" or "good girl" trip on you. To earn this badge you repressed all the natural parts of yourself that didn't fit the blueprint (more of this later on). But you developed strong Not-OK feelings because you knew of the "bad" parts hidden within.

Your parents may not have been critical but were simply uninvolved with you. They left you basically on your own or shuffled you off to others for care. Your Child may then have reasoned, "I'm not worthy of their involvement."

The central point to remember is that

> **The amount of Not-OKness you live with
> equals the amount of
> criticism, controlling or uninvolvement
> you lived with.**

Your "Worthless, Unacceptable Me" came then from your Child reactions to any of these negative influences. It literally cannot exist once you dump the messages housed in the Critical, Controlling or Uninvolved Parent tape. Be aware that

> **Not-OKness is the cause of
> low self-esteem . . . your unfree Self.**

Your Adult tape

A third personality part—the Adult—develops as you come in contact with your world. Adult here does not mean grown up. Rather, it is the "thought" part of your personality.

It is that part capable of rational thinking, in touch with reality, that postpones a present pleasure for a long-term gain. It estimates the probability of the consequences of certain acts. It is the part of you that is responsible to yourself and others. The Adult is the seat of choice. It is, as you can see, an important part of the integrated, whole person.

Basically, then, you have "taught," "thought" and "felt" parts within. Each one can be turned on (moved to the center of your stage) when you speak, think or act . . . whether to yourself or others. And each part can take over your whole personality—either fleetingly or consistently. The chart on the next page illustrates your personality parts and their identifying traits.

Do keep in mind that the Child-in-you, regardless of your age or strength, always feels like a child. When it comes up front, it feels *needy* and *helpless*. It needs protection and reassurance even when life is peaceful. It may need firm but not harsh limits set for it. There are times when it does not know how to cope. Then it needs the Inner Nurturer and Adult-in-you to take over and figure out the answers.

As you continue reading you will see how to protect and nurture this Inner Needy Child. Remember it will be with you until the day you die and it will need the services of your Adult and Nurturing Parent for the ongoing support of a Self care system.

Personality structure

A diagram of the personality of the low self-esteemer or the self-doubter looks like this:

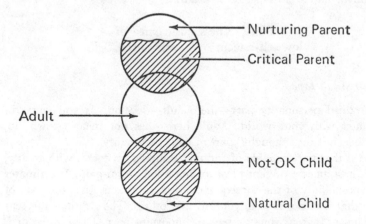

The more extensive your Critical Parent programming, the lower your feelings of self-worth. And the greater your vulnerability to stress. Your capacity to make responsible Adult choices is correspondingly lessened.

YOUR PERSONALITY PARTS

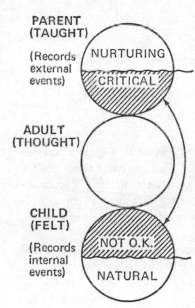

PARENT (TAUGHT)

(Records external events)

NURTURING

Empathic, demonstrates, explains, models, reacts, shares power, appreciates, sees what's *right,* manipulates environment not child. Teaches, "you are separate from behavior." Provides firm, not harsh, structure, limits.

CRITICAL

Judges, punishes, high demands, faultfinding, keeps power, controlling, sees what's *wrong.* Teaches, "you are what you do." Gives pain. Or uninvolved. Excessive or no limits or structure.

ADULT (THOUGHT)

Rational thought, in touch with reality, postpones present pleasure for long-term gain, probability estimator, *responsible* to self and others. The chooser. Keeps options open.

CHILD (FELT)

(Records internal events)

NOT O.K.

Helpless, hurt, deprived, rebellious, guilt-ridden, inadequate, "bad," unlovable. Tied to Critical Parent tape. (Feeds on Critical Parent messages.) Victim of Critical Parent voice. Receives pain.

NATURAL

Free, intuitive, playful, spontaneous, *impulsive,* creative, open to and expressive of feelings. Wants what it wants when it wants it—now.

The high self-esteemer's personality structure, on the other hand, looks like this:

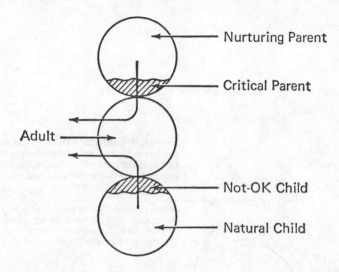

The high self-esteemer, you notice, has little negative programming and consequently few Not-OK feelings. Note the arrows in this diagram. They indicate that both the Nurturing Parent and Natural Child urges are available for use but are put through the Adult's contact with reality. As we've mentioned, this is not the case for the low self-esteemer.

High self-esteemers invariably have a fully functioning Adult. This means they are in touch with the natural consequences of their acts. And they have a commitment to being responsible. They choose constructive ways to let their Nurturer and Impulsive Child out but not at their own or others' expense.

For example, the sudden urge for a three-month trip to Europe might nurture you and please your Impulsive Child. Yet if such a trip would cost you your job and you want to keep it, if it would leave you swamped with debts or deprive those financially dependent on you, you do not act on this impulse. Instead you work out a self-renewal period that is more in line with reality and is not detrimental to yourself or others. Or you work out such an extended trip to no one's disadvantage.

In the high self-esteemer no one Voice (the Nurturer, Adult or Natural Child) exclusively silences the others. Each operates harmoniously and in contact with the others. Stress is more easily handled as a constructive challenge.

We can now see more clearly why the self-love of the high self-esteemer is not conceit. (Discussed in Chapter One.) The self-centered person lets his Impulsive Natural Child rule his life. He does whatever pleases him momentarily, regardless of the consequences to himself or others. He does not use his Adult or Nurturer.

Our focus

If you know TA, you've probably primarily thought about your tapes from the standpoint of how you and others relate.

Here, however, we shall look at them in terms of *how you relate to yourself—in terms of your own self-talk. For how you talk to yourself—what you do to yourself within—makes the difference between joy and pain.*

Many people who are or have been into TA see the Parent tape as a negative Voice. "She's coming on Parent" is clearly a no-no in their eyes.

I make a sharp distinction between the Critical Parent Voice and the Nurturing Parent one. As will become increasingly clear, I am convinced our own Inner Child needs the empathy, protection and emotional support of our Internal Nurturing Parent. If you don't have a sufficiently strong Inner Nurturer, you'll learn here how to develop one.

Before considering the steps to freedom, it is essential to be clearly aware of the power of your Not-OK Child tape. It came into being when you were very young. And it has been experienced as an integral part of you. It is experienced as a central "Truth" about your Being if your self-worth is low or shaky.

Let's see why and how this culprit affects your life.

· FOUR ·

THE POWER OF NOT-OKNESS

The Child's reality

Rationally you may find it hard to believe that if you are a doubter or loser, you are choosing that route. Why would any sane person do that?

When we're small our parents are seen as gods. Their view of us *is* our reality. So, if at a later age we try to see ourselves in a different light, we disobey the firmly entrenched parental view. Indeed, we fly in the face of what our Inner Child believes is reality. The Child-in-us finds it incomprehensible to challenge the view of the gods.

You are rare indeed if you had parents, teachers and friends completely free of hang-ups. They each saw you through eyes distorted by their own particular needs. These distortions prevented their seeing the Real You. But, once again, the Child-in-you cannot comprehend this.

Fred's parents were too involved with their own needs to be involved with him. His Inner Child reasoned, "I am not worth being involved with." His feelings of low self-worth came about because even as an adult he used their non-involvement as proof of his unworthiness.

Jill's parents gave approval only when she was living up to their overly high standards for achievement. As an adult she could only feel "good" inside if she piled up one achievement after another.

The excessive criticism Frank received as a child from his father became his own relentless criticism of himself as an adult. Just as he could never please his dad, he could never please himself (his Internalized Critical Parent).

As a present-day adult, then, in terms of intrinsic worth, you see yourself largely through borrowed Parent-tape eyes.

The past view of others is your present yardstick.

If your Not-OK taping has been strong enough, you behave, as we've mentioned, in self-defeating ways. To succeed in life or relationships would be at odds with that Internalized Critical Voice saying, "You are a loser." Beneath the loser's fear of failure is an even greater fear—fear of success.

Succeeding would mean giving up the only identity you have known. The very identity on which you have based your life. Only by courting failure and bringing it about can you be right about your negative self-image. Only by focusing on your shortcomings can you defend your Not-OKness. Remember, *your whole sense of identity is tied to that belief*. To your Inner Child that belief is what is real. Any other view is unreal. No wonder the Child-in-you clings stubbornly to what "seems" true.

The known is better

Your past scripting, no matter how painful, is known, predictable territory. We human beings take a jaundiced view of change. The Child-in-you reasons,

"The kind of climate I grew up in is the only kind worth having."

The particular shrivelers the Child is used to are familiar—regardless of how uncomfortable they have been. So it concocts, collects and clings to unpleasantness.

Imagine having lived in the Arctic as an Eskimo for the first twenty years of your life. Then you move to the desert. You would doubtless do everything to set up a frigid climate in your home—air conditioning, ice cubes, the works. You would avoid the sun's warmth at all costs.

Just like the Eskimo, your Inner Child goes after what it is used to. Since the Self you are aware of when you think of your worth is the Child Self, it seeks the same proportion of pain or comforts experienced in your past. Why? To re-establish the old familiar climate in your present-day situation.

Medical studies show that if too many major changes take place within a two-year span—even if they are positive changes—80 per cent are likely to become physically ill or have accidents. Change of any kind is stressful. It thrusts us into the unknown. So if discomfort is familiar (and it is to the loser and doubter) your Inner Child will prefer the comfort of discomfort simply because it is familiar.

If you continue to prove you're a louse, you don't have to change your script, your identity. Again, you avoid the threat of another change. If you play Victim, you hold onto your "Helpless Me"—a long-time, well-known friend.

One young man clearly stated this discomfort with change when he came into the counseling hour saying, "You know things have been peaceful this week. I haven't made chaos for myself. But I feel tension building inside. It's like I can literally feel myself working up to cause trouble for myself. I've lived with chaos for so long that non-chaos is really uncomfortable."

If we look at his comments in terms of his personality parts, we see his Not-OK Child literally feeling deprived when all is well. It is not getting the "oxygen" it needs to keep functioning. For his Not-OK Child the "oxygen," of course, is chaos, conflict, pain. If discomfort doesn't come, he (the Child-in-him that is used to chaos) feels driven to get some going. It demands center stage. It needs the familiar psychological climate. Neurotically, he (his Sad/ Bad Kid) needs pain even though his Adult rational mind does

not want it. An added payoff for seeking pain is that he doesn't
need to change his self-picture of Victim.

His Not-OK Child Voice carries the greatest weight. It clamors
loudly for its "food." Unaware of other options, he unintentionally
gives its claims the power to rule his life. Be aware that

> **Your Not-OK Child
> is out to rule you.
> But you hold the power
> of whether to give in
> to its demands or not.**

In general, the low self-esteemer has received more negative than
positive messages in childhood. If this fits for you, then your pain-
giving and pain-receiving tapes will go center stage at every opportunity. The self-doubter has received conditional inputs as to worth
from his or her past. "*If* you . . . , then you can earn your value"
has been the message. So the doubter lives with pain when he or she
isn't living up to the conditions required in earlier days. The high
self-esteemer has had fewer shrivelers sent his or her way and has
experienced having value without forever having to earn it.

Who rules your life?

Because the Child "I" houses internal feelings toward the Self,
programmed in your earlier years, it can rule your life if you let it.

Would you allow a demanding, tempestuous, unruly youngster to
literally take over your life? Order you around? Continually cause
painful destruction for you?

"Not me," you say.

Each of us needs to check that the Child-we-once-were is *not*
running our lives today. Its irrational fears, need for pain or un-
willingness to heed reality can dominate our stage. Such checking
means relentlessly asking ourselves, "To whom am I giving my
power? Which 'I' rules my life? Who gets star billing: the Persecu-
tor, Victim, Rebel, Martyr, Loser, Doubter?"

Simply identifying the culprit is the first step. How to move it
from power will be our central focus as we go along.

Closeness brings hurt

As a very young child you were enormously vulnerable. You came into the world with few devices to protect yourself. You could move toward the pleasurable, pull back from the painful and you could cry.

If as you reached out for close contact with others, you were ignored, disrespected or punished, you learned to fear psychological intimacy. No matter now that your Nurturer, Adult and Natural Child want closeness. The Rejected Child-in-you will hold back. It still believes that survival depends on distancing. The memory of its original helplessness—the vulnerability that resulted in pain—cautions, "Don't get close. You'll get hurt. And you deserve rejection."

Your Inner Child *can make you believe you are as vulnerable today as you were long ago.* If a loved one leaves you now, you may experience the same devastating abandonment that you would have if your mother left you when you were two. Your Totally Dependent Child has moved to center stage.

Once Not-OKness is established as true for you, fear of closeness is further reinforced by this line of thinking: "If I let others know the real 'Me' they too will discover I'm Not-OK, and they'll surely reject me. More of that I need like a hole in the head. So it's best to hide rather than be known."

If your childhood parent seemed too powerful, your fear of closeness may have spawned from a fear of fusion, a fear of having no identity apart from that parent, a fear of disappearing. To you getting close means being gobbled up. Or at best being a mere appendage.

Although most of us think we want closeness, for far too many of us, the Inner Child has learned to be leery, if not downright frightened, of it.

Your Child is dependent

When you were very young, you had no choice as far as being dependent was concerned. Your very survival depended on others meeting your physical and psychological needs. You literally had to

be done for by others. So it was logical that much of your energy
went into manipulating others to meet your needs.

Your parents may have needed a dependent child or a "patient."
As long as you played that part you held their attention and kept
them involved with you. You froze at the Helpless level to avoid rejection.

Many come to adulthood with unmet dependency needs or with
programming that has sanctioned playing the Weak Child. Then
you unconsciously refuse to use your own inner resources. It's as if
the Child-in-you doesn't recognize that the you-of-today has the
choice to lean on others to do for you or the choice to do a great
deal for yourself.

The Child tape simply feels helpless about its helplessness. If
given a loud enough Voice in your inner dialogue, it does not recognize that

What was true
in the past
is no longer true.

Giving up loser dependency means you don't ask others to do "it"
for you. You don't wait for others or circumstances to "save" you.
You welcome help and ask for it when it's genuinely needed. But
you take an *active* part in getting your needs met through your own
efforts. You refuse to play Helpless. That's what growing up inside
is all about—becoming self-responsible and dropping controller-
controllee games.

Real payoffs for your Not-OK Child come then with keeping this
pain-inflicting, self-limiting tape active:

1. it doesn't have to change its "Unacceptable" identity—
   the "Me" it has built;
2. the Inner Child keeps the blend of hurts and negatives
   it's been used to—it lives with the comfort of the known;
3. your Not-OK Child avoids getting close to others, a situation past experiences have proved dangerous;
4. your Inner Child doesn't give up dependency, which
   means it doesn't have to exert itself; and

5. it doesn't risk rejection of those dependent on its weaknesses.

What a powerful array of reasons your Not-OK Child has for
being a loud and noisy speaker in your internal dialogue! Its Voice
literally screams, "Danger! Survival depends on your listening to
me." It has strong vested interests in dominating your stage. And it
will resist having its convictions challenged with all the power at its
command.

Releasing illusions

Easing the Not-OK Child from your internal cast of characters
means questioning its assumptions. Its beliefs are heavily based on
the preschooler's magical and distorted view, as we've seen. Amazingly, you will find that

All you give up
are its illusions.

You give up its *illusion* that the pain of the past is known and
therefore preferable.

You give up its *illusion* that those who rejected originally were
omniscient . . . that they saw you accurately.

You let go of its *illusion* that you put together the package called
"Me" accurately.

You release its *illusions* created by false programmings—untruths
you've based your life on.

You give up its *illusion* that you have no choice.

Peggy, for example, became aware that she featured her Inner
Child's Victim Voice.

"I noticed that I *gravitated* toward people who were just as critical as my mom. When they dished out blame I bought it whether it
fit or not. A part in me believed that others saw more clearly than I
did, so when they picked at me, I figured I deserved it. I never
stood up for myself because in the past it only brought trouble.

"When I became aware that Poor Peggy was always out front, I
decided to exercise my power of choice. I asked for a transfer when

an opening came up to work for a guy who everyone said was neat to work for. At first when he complimented me for some work, I found myself not believing him. But I told myself that I'd spent too many years believing what was wrong; it was time for letting in some positives because part of me did see that my work was OK.

"If a guy I dated came on with a lot of criticisms, I told myself, 'Peggy, you don't need that any more,' and I dropped him. I stopped believing that I had no choice in the friends I had. And I made a very definite, conscious effort to be friendly with people who had positive attitudes and treated me with respect.

"It didn't happen overnight. But by really asking myself how I set myself up for pain, I became all too aware that I did just that. It meant that for the first time in my life I started taking the initiative to put myself into positive situations. I asked myself almost daily, 'Does this situation or person build me up or tear me down?' If it was a downer I got out of it. At first it seemed strange but it doesn't any more. I've started believing in me. And I realized that if I didn't respect myself, no one else would."

Giving up illusions can feel decidedly scary, especially when they form the basis of your identity. The feeling is not unlike suddenly losing your sight. You are thrust into functioning from a totally new and different perspective.

In addition to going into the unknown, when you dump these illusions you've lived with so long, the Child-in-you may feel as if it is destroying the real parent. No, you only do away with dependence on untruths which have *seemed* to be truths.

You can expect your Not-OK Child to use every trick in the book to keep from being moved out. After its storminess, it usually does some weeping. You may experience grief in giving up this long-familiar but outworn part in you.

Allow the "Unacceptable Me" that is being dismissed to mourn. (How to do this is discussed in Chapter Six.) Hear it out but know that its replacement will be an infinitely superior tenant in your House of Self. You will be transplanting your "Me" into nurturing soil and experience the joy of blooming.

Your Helpless Child, fearing abandonment, will need reassurance that your Nurturer will stand by to protect and meet its needs. It will no longer be dependent on an outside nurturer because you will be laying claim to the Nurturer Within. We'll see how to do that in later chapters.

Are you driven and controlled by old past tapes? Or do you claim your right to free choice? You answer these questions each moment of your life. Know it or not, you choose how to direct your life.

The blame game

You may say, "I did not choose my negative childhood experiences. So how can I be choosing today? I'm a victim of my past."

It is true you didn't choose non-nurturing soil as a child. It is true that your feelings of inadequacy were learned from the person-to-person climate you grew up in. This makes it very easy to say, "I wouldn't be unhappy today if it weren't for my parents (or others) who made me feel so inadequate."

Let's look squarely at the issue of blame. If I sit and play "If-it-weren't-for-them," there are real payoffs for me. By blaming others for my present unhappiness, I overlook some important realities.

First, every parent and teacher does the best he or she can at any given moment in view of their past experiences, inner and outer pressures, needs and hang-ups. That best may or may not have met my emotional needs.

Secondly, nurturing is like feeding. If others had little or nothing in their cupboards and I was hungry, they could not adequately feed me. Before blaming, I need to be aware that the only reason some significant person charged with nurturing me fell short is that someone in that person's life did not stock his or her cupboard with "goodies." That person's bucket was empty in some way and he or she was unaware of this lack. What they did not give me, *they did not have to give because of their own lacks or deficits.*

Finally and most important, if I blame others and weep over the shrivelers ladled out, I cling to my dependent Victim game. I have the perfect copout: I don't have to exert myself. Until I do, I am still tied to the view of past others.

The inner push-pull

In each of us there is one part that wants to grow up. There is another part that does not want to grow up. The truth is that the

Dependent Child-in-us simply does not want to claim its own power. It wants to give it away, or manipulate others with it.

An honest statement of this situation would be, "I do and do not want to grow up. I do and do not want to make nice for me. I do and do not want to be responsible for my own growth."

The reward for choosing self-sufficiency, of course, is that you move from being a pawn to others' whims to being the captain of your own ship.

New energy

Not the least of the advantages to giving up your pain-producing inner dialogue will be a marked increase in energy.

You might think for a moment of each of your tapes as being like a separate motor in a multi-motored car. Each motor draws from a central gasoline tank. Naturally gasoline used by motor A is not available for motors B, C, D or E.

You and I, of course, don't use gasoline to run on. Instead, we use energy. And the energy siphoned off by the Critical Parent and Not-OK Child "motors" is unavailable for use by the Nurturing Parent, Adult and Natural Child "motors." This means less energy for nurturing Self and others, less energy for rational thinking and spontaneous joyful living, less energy to develop your assets. You know yourself when you are deeply worried, for instance, you have less energy to work effectively at a particular task or for simply having fun.

A universal phenomenon happens when you noticeably reduce self-criticism (Critical Parent) and feelings of inadequacy (Not-OK Child). You suddenly find you have all kinds of new energy. That energy has been there all along. It has simply been drained off to support the activity of these two destructive personality parts.

Unused tapes

As we saw in the personality structure diagram if you live a self-destructive or self-defeating life you may literally leave whole parts of your personality unused. You leave some of your "motors" idling.

Mary does not use her Critical, Nurturing, Natural Child or

Adult tapes. She plays Totally Dependent Child, expecting everyone to service her. Bob plays Total Controller or he won't play at all. He only relates to people who let him dominate. He rejects all who have a mind of their own. His way is the only way.

Some people feature one tape exclusively in one setting and reserve another exclusively for a different setting. Sam plays Total Adult at work, where he deals primarily with numbers and ideas. But at home he flips; he majors in Dependent Child. Pat largely relates to acquaintances outside her family from all her tapes. But in close relationships she largely plays Controller.

If you have some addiction (it matters not whether that compulsion is for alcohol, drugs, gambling, overwork, overpleasing or overeating), you live with excessive self-criticism and guilt. Because of a vested, programmed interest in collecting ammunition against yourself, your gasoline-energy is rationed out almost exclusively to the Critical Parent and Not-OK Child Voices.

If you are "addicted," you are ordinarily a "super" person: super sensitive, super perceptive, super bighearted, super masked, super self-indulgent, super self-critical, super vulnerable to stress. You may likely be super gifted with unusual degrees of talent that you steadfastly deny possessing.

The irrationality of your compulsion—the consequences of its effect on you and others—is vehemently denied. You do not let in nurturing nor evidence of your worth. Why? Because your Adult and Self nurturing tapes are turned off. Committed to self-ruination, it is logical to keep them turned off. You live with a strong learned injunction against winning. The issue is not

What drives you
but who drives you?

Freedom to be your own person is out since *you've not developed an identity apart from Not-OKness.* You've never really been introduced to the Real You.

Compulsive addictions only mean a programmed commitment to pain and failure. You live with a "mustness," a drivenness toward solutions that don't work in your best interest. Your Not-OK Child is given top billing. Because of your often unconscious blame-guilt self-dialogue you blindly follow the inner directive that screams, "Lose!"

If you are dependent on an anti-life addiction, you can switch your compulsion to a pro-life one. Members of Alcoholics, Overeaters, Narcotics, Parents Anonymous have remarkable success by simply shifting their dependency from negative addictions to dependence on a Higher Power. You can choose to become positively addicted to jogging, painting, singing, meditation or whatever once you give up your need to do yourself in. You remain compulsive. But you choose a positive outlet for your compulsion.

The good news that you don't have to remain trapped cannot be overemphasized. Freedom is yours for the choosing.

"On automatic"

Most doubters and losers think they are "doing their own thing." Literally they are captives "on automatic." Daily they grind out Not-OK solutions that entrap. Like robots, they are totally controlled by past programming. Their lives are predictably monotonous round trips, not adventuresome journeys.

Early in life Jack concluded he was a failure. His father deserted the family and refused to have anything to do with him. Having lost in winning his father's acceptance and being reared in great poverty, Jack operated on a loser tape. Automatically (yet unconsciously) he set himself up to lose.

Although extremely bright and competent, he always managed to get to work late. He refused to follow company rules. Eventually he was fired. He set up his own business at enormous financial sacrifice—even mortgaging his home. Just as his fledgling shop started to operate in the black, he sold it at a real loss and started in a new venture for which he had no talent.

His frantic wife insisted he get personal therapy. But no sooner did he begin to make progress there than he quit therapy. In desperation his wife left him. Vocationally, financially and emotionally his Inner Child directed all his choices. The familiar climate of failure and abandonment were automatic themes he played out in adulthood. He allowed his past conditioning to rule his life. He consistently avoided solutions that would work in his best interest.

Why? To keep his Inner Child in the climate it was used to. Pain, failure, abandonment.

The problem is that long after we leave the influence of those who programmed us (they may even be dead), we keep their instructions ruling our lives. Originally we sucked in their Voices and modeling. Then through lack of awareness *we* keep reindoctrinating ourselves by playing their tapes in our heads. Once it was others who made us feel "bad." Now we take over the job by *parenting ourselves with their phantom talk.*

Who you think you are then has resulted from your programming. Today's pain comes from imitating Voices from your past. To increase your self-esteem you do not need to change your Real Self; instead,

You need to change your Belief System about yourself.

The basic issue is not what happened in the past, but rather where you are today and what you decide to do about your self-talk. Are you "on automatic"? Are you a slave to old tapes and child-born illusions? Or are you free of an inappropriate and worn-out Belief System?

Power or love

The Critical Parent and Not-OK Child Voices are absorbed with the *love of power*—the need to control, manipulate, win, be right. A great struggle is waged over who reigns.

The Nurturing Parent, Adult and Natural Child Voices are concerned with the *power of love.* Becoming a high self-esteemer means casting your vote in favor of the power of love over the love of power.

Then you don't approach others with that great needful yet often camouflaged cry, "See me with the 'I' of love. Tell me I count." This Child anguish is replaced by the Nurturer's quiet encouragement for Whole Self celebration. And when you affirm yourself and know that you count, you see the beauty in others—through the outer to the inner. You give up needing and relish affirming.

When Mike and Ann reduced their negative tapes, he shifted from playing Power Holder and she gave up playing Powerless. Now their energies were focused on co-operating with and affirming each other's growth rather than being channeled into a never-ending power struggle. They respected the integrity of the other as well as their own. Conflicts were negotiated in a climate of caring rather than in the earlier one of dominance-submission.

The job to be done

To move from low to high self-esteem—to free the Real You—your task will be

1. to shrink your Internal Critical Parent, which dramatically reduces your Not-OK feelings;
2. to deal with these negative tapes constructively when they clamor to be heard;
3. to increase Self nurturing and allow your Natural Child to expand;
4. to activate your Adult through awareness that you can choose to put yourself in the winner's circle; and
5. to make contact with the Real You—your Essential Being.

To remain a pawn to past conditioning is one choice. With strong Critical Parent and Not-OK Child tapes, you will tend to play out your life mechanically. Life and others will push your "hot" buttons and you'll automatically come up with a programmed reaction that causes pain. You will not be free.

To move clear of past conditioning is another choice. You eliminate the negative programming that causes discomfort for you and others. Then you are free to direct your own life. You don't function inwardly or outwardly as a machine but rather as an autonomous, whole person.

Either way, you cannot avoid choosing. The power of decision—to be a pawn to past conditioning or to be free of it—rests with you.

To begin with think of each tape or Voice as a character or person in your personal drama. See yourself as both the stage director and the playwright with the power to decide who gets what lines and who gets center stage. You can move your characters around, rescript them, decide who speaks when and where.

What follows is a set of instructions on how to reconstruct the package you call "Me." You will be directly challenging all the past negative inputs you used to construct a detrimental self-image. You will consciously become your own positive self-image architect. You will design a new House of Self so that You move with grace and ease. Last but not least, you will see how to move past your "Me" package to make contact with the Real Dweller within.

If you are ready to start, see following page.

PART II

THE PATH TO FREEDOM

My hope is that you will approach this section as you would a smorgasbord. Take what appeals to you and leave the rest behind at this time.

The ideas you most resist may often be ones that most imprison you. Give yourself permission to deal with them after you've mastered those you feel less resistant about.

On the other hand some may not apply at all in your case. They are challenges you don't need to work on. But check each one over by observing your inner dialogue before eliminating it from your "areas for growth" plan.

FIVE

WATCH YOUR LANGUAGE

The crucial questions

Knowing about your "thought," "taught" and "felt" parts gives you a handle on where you are with yourself today. If you think about the collection of put-downs that came your way in the early years, you know why your self-worth needs building up.

**But knowing why
is not enough.**

Knowing why does not free you. The crucial questions to zero in on are:

How do *I* keep myself unhappy?
How do *I* keep my pain going?
How do *I* keep myself stuck replaying the same worn-out tunes?

When you gave up crawling to start walking as a toddler, you made a dramatic shift in how you got around. The simple shift from all fours to upright opened up all kinds of possibilities for you.

Once we quit putting responsibility "out there," once we truly shift our focus to these questions, we make the dramatic shift to self-responsibility—the hallmark of the high self-esteemer.

It is not enough then to be able to identify your destructive tapes —*the "I's" giving or absorbing pain.* You need to know how to eliminate them—to defuse their power in your life. First you need to see how you keep your life bleak by using them. And then you need to reprogram your tapes actively so they work *for* instead of *against* you.

Do you find yourself balking at the mere suggestion that you and not others are causing your pain? *Most people do.*

Two suggestions. Either hold on to your resistance and keep reading. See if that resistance gradually melts. Or think of some person you know who is obviously messing up his or her life and mentally apply the ideas to this person for your first reading.

Self-parenting

You and I continually parent ourselves. In a real sense through our own self-talk we are either in the construction business or the wrecking business.

The idea that you are parenting yourself may be a brand-new one for you. But mull it over and listen to how you talk to yourself. See yourself as a little Objective Observer seated inside yourself, arms folded and tuned in to the kind of talk and feelings going on. After you've collected this data, seriously ask yourself,

> ### "What kind of a parent
> ### am I
> ### to myself?"

Word watching

The first and simplest place to start in sorting out your answer to this question is to become familiar with the difference between Critical and Nurturing Self talk.

Your Critical Parent is perhaps most easily recognized by its use of certain words. When you hear yourself use them on yourself, consciously choose to switch to Nurturing words. (We'll look at both types momentarily.) Become a word watcher. For the essence of increasing your self-worth—the key to freedom—lies in knowing that

You can choose to be your own Nurturing Parent.

You rarely heard a Nurturing Voice? You only heard the opposite? OK. Here's your chance to reprogram your Parent tape. You can do it yourself.

Remember in Chapter Three we saw that the Critical Parent Voice is the top sergeant type. It's bent on overcontrol. It shoves people around with all kinds of blueprints . . . commands as to how you "should" behave, think, feel. It is the opinionated, learned, "must" voice that seeks to manipulate the Child-in-you. Whenever you hear yourself using certain words in your self-talk, you automatically know your Top-dog is "on." These words are "have to," "should," "ought," "must," "got to."

These words signal that one part in you is handing down edicts to another part. Such words eliminate free choice, self-responsibility, and set up a master-slave relationship within. They mean that one part doesn't believe in the other part. They carry the flavor of mild or severe scoldings or spankings, red-penciling the "Bad Child." These admonitions are like little hailstones beating down good feelings about yourself.

Destructive "should's" vs. code of ethics

Certain of society's "should's" are basic rules made to protect the rights of all. The person with no conscience, no sense of right or wrong—the psychopath—feels no commitment to a code of ethics. When he transgresses it's no skin off his teeth.

Some "should's" go to make up what we call a healthy conscience. And the high self-esteemer operates within a code of ethics. If he transgresses, he does not beat himself with never-ending guilt. Rather he owns up to the transgression, apologizes and makes restitution when it's possible. He is willing to accept the responsibility for his behavior. He may talk out his feelings of regret or turn to the law or his church to work out those regrets constructively. And then he lets the matter rest.

I want to make it clear that I am not talking about such "should's," be they traffic laws or the moral "should's" of positive religious conviction. If you only use these you are probably not lowering your self-esteem. "I should not steal," "I must not cheat on my income tax" are not the "should's" that do you in. It is the common garden variety of "should's" that we daily beat ourselves with. Here are some examples.

Garden-variety "should's"

Start today and make a conscious decision to be aware of your "shoulditis." How often do you find yourself thinking or saying,

> I *should* have thought of that idea.
> I *should* have done a better job.
> I *ought* to be more organized.
> I *must* remember to . . .
> I *have to* get myself going.

If you're like most people, this talk goes on and on. After each single pelting how do you feel? Guilty? Add up the number of Top-doggings you give yourself daily and multiply it by 365 (days in the year). Then ask yourself, "Who is making me feel so inadequate? Who keeps pouring in these messages that produce guilt?"

The should-ought-must Voice is tied to expectations others have programmed into us. And the lower your self-worth, the more loudly this Voice clamors for the impossible. Perfection in all things is its ideal, of course. If your Critical Voice is strong, it makes sure your Not-OK Child gets swatted every time you fall short of that ideal. (More of this in the next chapter on expectations.)

Non-control self-talk

Are you wondering how you can be true to your Adult Voice (the part that estimates the consequences of your acts, that is responsible to self and others) if you drop your garden-variety "should's"?

You can send yourself the same general message *without* peppering your self-worth with buckshot. You simply switch to words like "want to," "choose," "prefer," "wish" or "desire." Such words are Adult, Nurturing and Natural Child—not Critical. (It may sound like hairsplitting to suggest shifting from master-slave self-talk to choice or freedom words. But for high self-esteem, this shift is essential.) Notice the difference here.

CONTROL TALK: (*Judgmental—Critical*)	NON-CONTROL TALK: (*Non-judgmental— self-responsible*)
I *should* have thought of that idea.	I *wish* I had thought of that idea (IMPLICATION: I would like credit for it. OR It seems obvious and one part of me wishes to deal with the obvious myself.)
I *should* have done a better job.	I *wish* I'd chosen to do the job better. (IMPLICATION: I own up to the fact that I am *responsible* for the caliber of my work. OR I would *prefer* not to have inconvenienced others because of this *choice*.)
I *ought* to be more organized.	I *prefer* to be more organized. (IMPLICATION: It would be to my advantage and I *choose* not to get in my own way.)
I *must* remember to . . .	I *want* to remember to . . . (IMPLICATION: It will be of help to myself/others when I make that *choice*.)

I *have to* get myself going.	I *choose* to get myself going. (IMPLICATION: I don't *want* to pay the penalty for procrastination.)
I *have to* go or I'll be late.	I *want* to go as I don't *choose* to be late. (IMPLICATION: I do not *want* to pay for the consequences of tardiness.)
I *ought* to read more.	I *wish* I *chose* to read more. (IMPLICATION: I accept the responsibility for my *choices*.)
I've *got to* change that habit.	It would be more *desirable* to handle that this way; I *want* to change how I react. (IMPLICATION: I accept the *responsibility* for my behavior.)

Which kind of talk do you specialize in? Start observing.

In each case the words in the left column only beef up guilt feelings. The implications of such talk brew Not-OKness rather than freedom and autonomy—adult responsibility.

The self-talk in the right column is a clear-cut reinforcement within yourself that you *are* responsible for your choices. With these words you claim self-responsibility. Do you notice that self-punishment, self-lecturing and self-blame are absent in these statements? This kind of talk *denies your Not-OKness the messages it needs to flourish.*

Using the right-column talk does not mean you sit back complacently. You desire and wish to grow and change, of course. But your self-talk takes the form of intent, of commitment, of being in charge of your own destiny. And that's what autonomy is all about. Such talk continually reminds you that you are the Chooser. Remember, the Critical Voice is one of control, blame and manipulation. The Nurturing and Adult Voices are ones of faith, inner choice and the acceptance of personal responsibility.

Choice and helplessness

As a small child you were originally helpless up against a critical or demanding parent and much of the world. That helplessness was experienced as "I can't." Today if your self-worth is low, you continue to tell yourself (and others) that you "can't." When you do, you feature your Helpless Victim tape. Let's see how accurate most "can'ts" are.

Make a list of all the things you say "I can't" to. A complete list. Go over it now and cross out every one of the "can'ts" that is actually a "won't." Of course every "won't" is an "I choose not to." And that is OK. We all have the right of choice, but we fool ourselves when we duck the responsibility for our choices, whatever they may be.

Your particular "can't" list might read:

I can't help myself.
I can't wear black.
I can't take heights.
I can't stand jazz.
I can't go without eight hours' sleep.
I can't quit smoking.
I can't stand up for myself.
I can't jump off a ten-story building without injury.

The only valid "I can't" is the last one. Each of the others is simply an "I choose not to" for whatever reason. Usually there is a price attached that I choose not to pay. And that is all right.

The point once again is: winners don't play Helpless Victim. Not even in their self-talk. They consistently claim their choices as their own.

When you and I do mental con jobs on ourselves we only limit ourselves. "Can't" means "physically unable to" and nothing else. *Refuse to use this word unless you are physically unable to do that thing.* Every time you hear yourself say "I can't" switch to "I won't" or "I choose not to" and get the feel for reclaiming your power of choice, your autonomy.

"But," you say, "I *can't* keep my mother from annoying me."

All right. Let's imagine that one way she annoys you is by criticizing. Everyone has the right to criticize if he or she wants to play that tape. It is not her act but *your reaction to her act* that is the problem. You can choose to let her do her critical number without hooking into it.

Naturally you wish she would not criticize, but she does. The problem is usually that you (the Child-in-you) want something else from her—like approval. But maybe for that moment or most of the time approving is not her game.

So you give her the space to do her dance; you *release* her to do her "thing." But you can choose not to bite the bait. You can choose to simply observe but you let the words flow over and past you. No one but you takes the hook; no one but you lets the words sink in.

Unfortunately, you and I cannot always control what anyone else does. But *we can choose our reaction*. When you say, "I can't keep my mother from annoying me," what you really say is, "I choose not to stay free of her games," or "One part of me (Not-OK Child) chooses to absorb the darts." *Beneath these statements is either the need to feel done in or the Child's past need for her approval.*

If you feel like throwing this book at me right now, I can thoroughly understand. The idea that we control our own reactions is one of the most difficult concepts to grasp at a gut level. The Child-in-us is an emotional reactor. When my Child, when your Child no longer *needs* others to respond as we would like (more of this in the next chapter), when we have released the other from meeting our needs, then we reclaim our power. We do not give it away and thereby remain the victim of the other.

"I can't help feeling depressed," is a common "powerless" statement. This sentence is more accurate when you say, "I choose to feel depressed."

I *know* when you're depressed it feels as if you are helpless against this feeling. It does not *feel* like a choice. But it is. Depression is preferred to facing other feelings or taking certain actions. If you doubt this, quickly fill in the following sentence:

"The good thing about feeling depressed is . . ."

Having trouble finding a payoff for depression? Keep pressing yourself for that payoff. Be brutally honest with yourself. You may find yourself finally answering, "When I'm depressed I don't let myself face how angry I truly am," or "I don't have to face how helpless I feel," or "I get to feel deprived and done in," or "I don't have to do anything for myself," or "I don't have to take a particular action I'm fearful of," or "I get sympathy."

Do you ever say, "I can't get myself going?" Insist on honest self-talk. Say, "I choose not to get myself going," and then look for the payoff that makes this a preferred choice.

You find yourself reluctant to use the new language of choice? The Child-in-you and me really resists this kind of talk. Remember, it does not want to grow up. The point is that we *are* responsible for our choices but this part in us does not want to claim that responsibility. Repeatedly and relentlessly we need to remind ourselves of this dynamic. Gradually, however, if you insist firmly and long enough, owning up to your choices will become habitual.

One reason we resist this kind of talk is that if we own up to the fact that we choose, we force ourselves to look squarely at *why* we continue self-defeating choices, and most of us don't want to look at that. (Remember, the "Unacceptable" Child Within is a powerful and subversive force.)

Secondly, if we can't blame others or some mysterious force that seems beyond our control, we begin to realize that to get what we *say* we want will mean *change* and *effort*. The easy way out is the Child-in-us wanting to play Copout.

Let's imagine that one of my goals is to do well in a class I'm taking. This means doing certain required reading. But I continually procrastinate and fail to do the work.

Rather than fool myself by saying, "I just can't get down to studying," I purposely say to myself, "I choose not to do the necessary reading." (Who else is doing the choosing?)

Most of us don't want to admit that we choose to set ourselves up to fall short. It's much easier to believe some invisible force or an innate laziness continually gets in our way.

Maybe I have other things on my mind so that concentration is difficult right now. (Then why am I not choosing to deal with these distractors so I am free to concentrate?) Maybe my procrastination is a rebellion against my parents' values. Maybe I have a loser tape that doesn't want me to succeed in reaching goals as that would go against my programmed Self Belief System. (Why am I not choosing to challenge a self-defeating way to rebel? Or to correct that false belief?) Maybe I'm a poor reader. (Why don't I choose to improve my reading skills?) Maybe I have chosen to take this class not out of genuine interest but to reach a goal to get someone else's approval. (Why do I choose to do that?)

Once I own up to choosing not to work, I am forced to look at what is going on inside me that makes not studying *the preferred choice*. By refusing to duck the fact that I choose I can more clearly search for the ulterior motive behind my choice. Disclaiming responsibility for my choice only means I pull the wool over my own eyes. And the Child-in-me wins again.

The answer I come up with may be as simple as "I'm interested in the class but not strongly enough to put out the required effort." Then I have clearly defined what has greater value for me. Obviously interest has second billing and energy expended has first billing. There is nothing wrong with such priorities except that, whatever the priority, I will pay for the consequences of my choices.

Next I consciously tap into my Adult by asking, "How will I feel in the long run? What is the price attached? Am I willing to pay that price? Which 'I' in me wants to pay it? Is it the 'I' that is for me or against me?"

It is all right to choose not to, but it is to my disadvantage not to look at the long-range price for avoidance. Each choice you and I make is a preferred one. Winners own up to their choices and act on nurturing, responsible ones; losers do not.

One psychotic patient became completely rational during the time he had pneumonia. Once his physical disease was over he returned to his psychosis. He needed a symptom to avoid coping with very trying relationships. When he had a physical excuse, he didn't need the psychological one.

A migraine sufferer unconsciously chose headaches when he needed to withdraw for a few days from stress. When he became aware of this choice and began to like himself better, he gave himself permission to lounge around for a few days when pressures built up. But now his withdrawal could be freely chosen without his having to spank his Not-OK Kid with a headache. He gave up needing a physical excuse along with learning less painful ways to handle his pressures.

It is rare when we are not the choosers. As Viktor Frankl points out so dramatically in *Man's Search for Meaning*, even in the Nazi prison camps one ultimate choice remained with each person. Each one could choose his or her attitude and reaction. No one can control your inner reactions and choices. You alone hold that power.

The idea that you choose your symptoms is hard to accept at first. But the next time you get a headache, back pain, asthma attack, rise in blood pressure, or the flu, ask yourself seriously, "What reward comes my way because of it? What gains—like attention or self-punishment—are in it for me? What is it I want to avoid? Was this the way I was programmed to handle stress? Am I operating off an old tape?"

Physical and psychological symptoms need treatment by those qualified, but they do serve a purpose. And they can be lessened or eliminated when you choose more constructive ways to meet your needs. More of this in Chapter Nine. Part of nurturing yourself means giving yourself permission to choose those ways.

A new language for self-esteem

A first step toward increasing your self-worth then lies in actively, consciously refusing to give your Critical Parent or Helpless Child Voices the power of center stage. Claim your right to choose nurturing self-talk. Watch your language carefully.

The words used in self-talk affect you fully as much as the food you eat. What kind of dialogue diet are you on?

As Mary said, "I choose not to 'should' on me any more." Paul said, "My two favorite words are 'I choose.'" And he lost forty-five pounds in six weeks by recognizing he chose to overeat to stuff down feelings of guilt and deprivation. He owned up to the fact that he purposely but unconsciously had made himself fat rather than face those feelings, deal with them constructively and actively meet his needs through his own efforts rather than waiting for someone to rescue him. He chose not to wall himself off physically any more.

"I'm astonished," said Bonnie, "at how I feel inside when I remember the simple switch from prison self-talk. I *really* do feel freer, more on top of things. We've made it a game at home; everyone who uses one of 'those' words forfeits a dime."

Part of self-affirmation means giving up the internal controller-controllee game. Love has no room for manipulation. You start on the path of being loving to you when you set it aside. Inner peace is more likely when controlling goes and free choice comes.

Applaud yourself each time you use the brand-new language. When you slip back (and you will, especially at first), just erase it and rephrase your self-talk. Remember the Nurturer knows that new growth and change come slowly. It accepts regression. It welcomes each bit of progress and understands backsliding.

Freeing yourself of master-slave self-talk may cause speech problems at first. But gradually it will become part of your inner dialogue.

A subtler form of Critical Parent control is found in the area of expectations. The next step along the freedom path means weeding out those expectations that make pain for you.

· SIX ·

EXPECTATIONS THAT CAUSE PAIN

Expectations and self-demands

When you were little a lot of silent and not so silent expectations came your way. Some were reasonable; some were not. It is the unreasonable demands that caused pain. They were the ones that asked for too much, too soon; the ones that cut across what you could comfortably handle at the time. Each carried a spoken or unspoken should-ought-must.

As a child you did not question their unreasonableness. You simply figured you were Not-OK if you couldn't clear the hurdles.

The *reasonable* expectations became part of your Nurturing tape. The *unreasonable* demands of others became part of the Critical Voice you use against yourself today.

Conversely, if little or nothing was asked of you, your Child may well have concluded, "Those others don't expect me to pull my weight because they think I'm pretty inadequate." Either extreme, too little or too much, in terms of what others expected feeds your Critical Self view.

Few of us grew up with expectations tailored precisely to our ability to handle them. So to a degree we can all profit from an honest inventory of our self-demands.

Perfectionism

The Critical Voice, as you remember, ladles out impossible ideals for acts, feelings, attitudes, thoughts and roles. It has no room for mistakes or fall-shorts. As long as its excessive demands rule your thinking, your Inner Child feels constantly driven to meet them. Or constantly driven to rebel. "Continually try," "Why try" or "I'll get back at them" can become the Child's theme song. Then drivenness, apathy, active or passive resistance set in.

If Pete's project has a single flaw in it, he sees it as a flop. Meg is mortified if there's a run in her hose even though the snag happened at work. In spite of his heart attack John insists on not taking vacations and putting in fourteen-hour days.

Myrna won't take up any activities even though many appeal. Her Inner Child is frightened since it knows she wouldn't excel right away. Brenda's house has reached the point of filth; it's her way of saying no to her Parental tape that verged on a phobia about germs.

None of these people is responding as an autonomous person. Rather, each gives a "computerized," automatic response. A learned reaction geared to agree with or defy the Internal Criticizer.

Much as your Adult knows there is no such thing as perfection, the Demander-in-your-head may lead you to set up this goal unconsciously.

Your parents may not literally have asked for perfection. But if their love was tied to how you behaved your Inner Child may have reasoned, "If I behave perfectly they won't reject me," "If I always look good, I'll prove my value." The meticulous performance of perfectionism is the end product of "if-then" programming.

The perfectionist concentrates then on performance. Without a gold star every time you turn around, your Not-OK Child truly believes it will perish. Far too many adults live off the perform-or-perish blueprint.

An insidious form of "if-then" taping occurred if your parents expected you to have only positive feelings. Negative ones brought censure.

Your feelings are basic to your identity. If you were taught that certain ones were unacceptable, you learned that you had some definitely unacceptable parts. They pooled together to add to your "Unacceptable Me." Your Belief System went like this:

"I am worth little or nothing because of my 'bad' feelings. Others have a right to look down on me. I must hide them because they will only bring on rightful rejection. But I'm helpless to change them. I long for Self confidence. But how can I be confident in the Bad-Feeling Me?"

The Impossible-demands-from-others tape that created the original "Something's wrong with me" feeling is the low self-esteemer's downfall. Now he guarantees his dim self-view by laying those same excessive demands on himself. To hold on to the familiar feelings of low self-worth, he "needs" perfectionistic standards.

To use perfectionism in deed or feeling as your admission ticket to worth sets you up for automatic failure. There's no way to win. A self-defeating, pain-producing operation tying up enormous energy, it brews continual guilt, fear and shame food for your Not-OK Child. If when you checked your should-ought-must talk you found such words frequent, you are probably a perfectionist.

The search for approval

The source of the perfectionist's self-expectations is the Child's once appropriate need for parental approval. Not having gotten it unless he danced to their tune, in adulthood he unconsciously turns all others into substitute parents. Since none of them is his parent, of course, he never makes it. But he blindly goes after the OK stamp from everyone for everything.

The mere thought of possible outer disapproval activates the Demander-within. To still that Voice he plays the exhausting Professional People-Pleaser role. Even if no one is around, he can't relax without feeling guilty. Why? Because the Criticizer-in-his-head is his constant companion. He is never free and forever dependent. The tragedy is that

To have everyone's approval
means giving up the Self.

Of course there are those who will try to put you in the service of their emotional needs. And they may well cry "Foul!" if you don't come through on all counts. If you need everyone's approval you choose to be a sitting duck for them.

If the other needs to persecute, she may elect you for the whipping post. But you are always free to decline the nomination once you cancel your commitment to self-pain and universal approval-seeking.

If the other needs to play martyr, he gasps hopelessly, but only changes tactics regardless of your sacrifices. More will be constantly demanded. His expectation that you play Rescuer is easier to release when you give up your need for universal acceptance.

Others may need to play self-destruct. You can open the door for competent help but in the final analysis only he or she can choose to walk through it. To put a "God trip" on yourself is unrealistic. Giving up "Everyone please love me" frees you from taking the dangled bait. Self-affirmation means you don't give others the power to manipulate you all over the map.

None of this means that you don't live in friendly co-operation with others or that you don't give to them where and when you comfortably can. But it is unrealistic to expect yourself to be a puppet born to please one and all. Freedom from the need for constant outer approval helps you remain true to your own integrity. Without inner integrity you really please no one.

If you've lived your life as a continual People-Pleaser, you may feel shaky at the thought of reclaiming self-territory. Keep in mind that your Scared Child dominates the stage at such times. Ask it what's the worst that can happen. Ask it if that worst is truly so devastating.

The popularity of Assertion Training classes is mute testimony to how many people are trying to kick the People-Pleaser tape. It isn't easy at first but it can be done. It needs to be done for high self-esteem.

Terry, for example, starts to apologize for her overdue book as she's paying the fine. She resists as she knows she had harmed no one and is handling the consequences responsibly.

Betty used to work herself into a tizzy to arrive on the dot. Now she allows herself ten or fifteen minutes leeway unless that will truly inconvenience her or others. She's even chosen to tell friends, "I'll be there at five, give or take a few." Carol has given herself permission to have a home with the "lived-in" look. With small children she was driving herself into tension headaches until she released her perfectionism and need for constant approval on every point. Cliff hands in competent reports but he's stopped straining to make each a masterpiece since that isn't called for on his job.

Check your behavior to see if you play Always Nice Kid. Do you live life as an apology, as a placater? Are you free to let others know when they've crossed your "ouch" line? Do you reserve the right to say "No"?

To get a feel for the difference between operating off the constant-need-for-others'-approval position vs. the self-affirming position, try this experiment.

Choose an hour or a day and consciously talk and relate to everyone you meet as if you had a desperate need for acceptance. Notice what you have to do and say when you live off this position. Notice the internal price you pay.

Follow this experiment with an hour or a day during which you continually relate to others with an inner conviction that you have worth and merit. You don't ride roughshod over others but you consciously walk, talk and work off self-confidence.

If that's not natural for you, act *as if* it is. Imagine being an actress or actor who feels solid self-worth and inner integrity. Play the part just for the experience. How do you behave differently? What does it feel like? How do the reactions of others differ? If you are working with this material in a group, share what you experienced in each situation.

Imperfection

Think of someone you know who always does everything right. She never has a hair out of place, never loses her cool, always has the perfect response. How do you feel around her?

Contrast these feelings with those you have when you are with someone who does make mistakes at times, who isn't always totally organized or on top of it. Chances are you feel more comfortable around him. Right? Most of us feel a bit threatened around Polly Perfect; she's hard to feel close to. Humanness, not perfection, is what we can relate to.

Betty blushingly shared this incident with a friend when she came for coffee.

"I'm so embarrassed I could just die! About ten-thirty this morning I answered the doorbell and there was a new neighbor collecting for the Arthritis Fund Drive. There I stood at that hour with my hair in curlers, a moldy old dirty bathrobe on and she could see through to my kitchen which looked like a disaster area. I cringe to think what she must have thought."

Her friend responded by asking, "I wonder how you'd have felt if you'd been the new neighbor collecting and you'd found her in that state at ten-thirty in the morning?"

Instantly Betty replied, "Oh, I would have felt such relief to know that she had those mornings too."

Have you ever thought you may actually be doing the other a favor—giving the gift of safety—by allowing him or her to experience your non-perfection? Try it. You'll like it. It's so much more enjoyable to be a human being with clay feet living among other imperfect people. Much more enjoyable than being a pretend model.

Joan and Ted were having an argument. Ted finally asked his wife why she was getting so angry at him.

"Well," said Joan, "I think what you said is just plain stupid!"

Ted laughingly replied, "Joanie, I reserve the right to say things you think are stupid." Ted didn't demand of himself that he always come on like Bob Brilliant. Do you reserve that right for yourself? If you are a Nurturing Parent to yourself, you allow yourself to be fallible, not to know it all, to be imperfect.

To continue demanding perfection of yourself because it once was the only way to get the approval so vital in childhood is to fall into the old trap: *what was once appropriate still is.* This false belief needs to be challenged repeatedly.

If perfectionism is your hang-up, here's a little silent chant you can constantly repeat to yourself. "I don't *have to* be perfect. It only pushes others away." Remember:

Wholehearted Self-acceptance
is not possible for the perfectionist.

Making mistakes

None of us likes to make mistakes. Yet we all do. Without exception everyone you meet has pulled some real boners and will do so again. But most of us feel red-faced when we do. Why? Because somewhere inside, branded indelibly in our consciousness, is *the expectation that we shouldn't,* born of *the need to look good.*

The Nurturing Voice gives you permission to be human. It avoids expecting the impossible. Unless the excessive demands of your Internal Criticizer are turned off, you cannot increase your self-esteem.

Winners do not believe their self-worth evaporates when they fall short because as we'll see in Chapter Eight, they separate their person from their behavior. They know their behavior will probably always leave some room for improvement. Losers, on the other hand, act as if they will drop dead if evidence of their humanity surfaces for others or themselves to see. There is a "dire catastrophe" flavor to the loser's goofs. He does not reserve for himself

The right to
be wrong.

Who among us cannot say that some of our greatest learnings have come from mistakes we've made? A mistake can teach us something we never forget; it spotlights an area for growth. As one student put it, "I'm not OK (meaning perfect); you're not OK (perfect); and that's OK (perfect)." Can you let yourself experience the perfection of your imperfection?

Nurturing yourself by accepting you will fail at times doesn't mean you don't try to avoid failures. But when they come you refuse self-judgment. An easygoing attitude prevails. You let past mistakes be just that—past. Your attitude is that yesterday ended last night. You recognize that there is a statute of limitations on past errors and refuse to wallow in self-punishment year after year.

If you have trouble releasing yourself from past mistakes, it simply means you have not forgiven yourself.

To forgive is to pardon. To be pardoned is to go free.

Many of us have been pardoned by others, the law or the church, but we steadfastly refuse to pardon ourselves. And that adds up to a refusal to set ourselves free from the past.

Self-blame is the Criticizer's means of keeping your Not-OKness actively virulent. Self-forgiveness is your Inner Nurturer's way of releasing you to high self-esteem, which invariably means welcoming your lack of perfection.

You recognize that whatever you did was the best you could do under your particular limitations at the time. Unless you forgive yourself you cannot operate in the present with freshness and freedom.

The biggest mistake
is clinging to past mistakes.

There is a place where you are perfect, however. We'll look at that in the last chapter.

Observe yourself carefully this next week. When you make a mistake, what's your inner reaction? Do you shame and scold yourself? Try to deny it? Apologize profusely as if it were an irrevocable and unpardonable sin? If so, practice the "kindly grandmother" stance with yourself. Then you are not overly indulgent nor are you harsh. You consciously erase your self-pelting. You face the mistake and calmly take corrective action.

Rearranging priorities

A subtle form of perfectionism comes with the self-demand for constant performance. No matter how much you do or how fast you go you never catch up. Of course not. The Criticizer is rarely satisfied. You are supposed to be everywhere at once, getting everything done—perfectly, of course. You see things to be done laying their claims on you simultaneously like this /// rather than one at a time, like this =====.

You kick that monkey off your back by asking yourself each day what is the one most important task that truly needs doing. Give that item priority number one. Set up your priorities knowing that no human being completes everything at once. Nor can everything be done in one hour or one day or sometimes even in one year. You take the whip out of your slave driver's hand by reminding yourself (switching on your Nurturer) of your human limitations.

The myth of the Special Case

Do you find yourself thinking along this line? "Others can goof but not me. I'm the only one who can't afford imperfection. I'm the only one who needs approval so much, who feels so alone or who is so undeserving. My 'Unacceptable Me' is worse than yours so I really have to look good." The myth of the Special Case is one way to feel special. We are special in our Awfulness.

No way. This line of thinking is pure fairy tale.

Try this experiment. Stroll around in an area crowded with people. Specifically notice as many separate individuals as you can. Imagine each wears a special sign around his or her neck. It carries the Inner Child message

> "Please love me; reassure me. Sometimes (or most of the time) I feel scared, lonely, anxious, uncertain."

Now imagine these same people dropping a cover over the Child message. This cover carries a different message. It reads,

> "I've got it made. I'm on top of it. See how strong, composed, powerful, angry, popular or aloof I am? Please notice this!"

This exercise in imagination lets you see how it really is for the vast majority of people you meet. The cover-up can fool you. Be aware that the game of Whistling-in-the-Dark is played by so many.

See through the second sign to the first one carrying the Needy Child message. Doing so helps you to

1. be less fearful of others;
2. relax and feel a common bond with them; and
3. give up the myth of being a Special Case.

Upsets and expectations

The next time you are upset, stop and pinpoint the expectation you just tripped over. Invariably you'll find one.

To spotlight the pitfalls an expectation inventory is needed. Write out a list of your expectations for your feelings, reactions, thoughts, skills, behavior, roles (man, woman, husband, wife, lover, child, friend, student, worker). Put those silent demands on paper.

Look what happened to Jill when she listed a few of her expectations for herself. "I *should* be calm, patient, in control, strong, organized, warm, friendly, generous, gentle, brave."

These were only a few of her self-demands. What did she do to herself when she felt rattled, impatient, irritated, weak, overwhelmed, disorganized, withdrawn, weak or cross?

She did the same thing to herself that you probably do. She felt "bad" and "guilty" and shamed herself righteously with her Inner Criticizer. Yet how can any of us be real and not experience some of the second feelings listed? It's impossible. Her ideal was not realistic.

Simply listing her self-demands gave her instant awareness as to how she made pain for herself. What does your expectation list reveal to you? If you're using this in a group, you may want to share what you learned from your inventory.

Now that you have written the list of expectations you lay on yourself, write out those you lay on others in your life. Then check to see how closely they match. You'll likely find that what you expect of yourself—realistic or not—is what you expect of others.

Now make a list of five things that consistently upset you whenever they occur. Your list might read this way:
I always get upset when

1. I'm asked to do something I don't like to do.
2. someone doesn't seem to appreciate a kindness I've extended.
3. the phone keeps ringing when I'm very rushed.
4. others don't co-operate.
5. something I've really looked forward to doesn't materialize.

Next look for the *unmet expectation behind each upset*. In the list above you can see that the expectations behind the upsets are as follows:

1. I *should* not be asked to do things I don't like. I don't want to face the other's disappointment or disapproval by refusing. I don't want the strain of meeting the request. I *expect* others to keep that pressure off me.
2. Others *should* appreciate my "good works" and give them recognition.
3. People *should* know better than to call when I'm busy, and/or I *must* answer the phone if it rings.
4. I *expect* others to co-operate always. (Your Adult mind may doubt this fits for you. But check by asking yourself when you last were truly accepting of lack of co-operation.)
5. If I anticipate an event with eagerness, it *should* be forthcoming. Life and others *should* not disappoint me.

This simple exercise can help you see that

**Behind every upset
there is
an unmet expectation.**

Once we clearly define what that expectation is, we often see our Controlling Criticizer or Demanding Child in full operation. Unreasonableness comes into sharper focus. Notice that each expectation is based on a "should."

It is highly profitable to work with your list of upsets and their underlying unmet expectations daily to get an ongoing feel for just how much you may keep yourself in turmoil. Remember, these silent unrealistic expectations are a clue that your negative tapes are on.

Next look over your upset list and see which one you'd be willing to give up. This sounds easy but you may humorously discover you don't want to give up any of them. If so, ask yourself why. Choose an easy one at first and consciously challenge the expectation behind it. Choose to let go of that expectation so that it no longer controls you. Once it no longer rules, try the same procedure with your next easiest-to-release one.

There is nothing wrong with expectations in and of themselves, but there's turmoil in them if you expect that you can always control their being met. You cannot. Those that are met are gravy. Those that are not can be seen for their unreasonableness. If they are not unreasonable you can deal with them appropriately. Handling upsets this way helps defuse their power over you.

What upsets us is not so much others and life but what we *expect* of others and life. It is extremely hard at first to get hold of the idea that we make pain for ourselves through our expectations, that we upset ourselves this way.

Being vs. having upsets

Notice the subtle difference between *being* upset and *having* an unmet expectation.

"I *am* upset because my car won't start." (This is *being* upset.) Now you wouldn't be upset unless your expectation was frustrated. It is more accurate to say, "*I have an expectation* that my car *should* start each time I need to drive it." (Here you face the *unmet expectation*. With the situation seen this clearly, it is obvious how unrealistic it is to expect that any piece of equipment will always work.) At this point you can choose to hold on to your unmet expectation or to release it.

Let's look at several common upsets from these two points of view.

Being upset:	*Having* an unmet expectation:
I *am* upset because my friend can't go.	I *have an expectation* that my friend's plans *should* mesh with mine.
I *am* upset because my husband watches TV too much.	I *have an expectation* that he *should* not watch TV so much.
I *am* upset because my wife is a messy house-keeper.	I *have an expectation* that my wife *should* not be a messy housekeeper.
I *am* upset because my suit came back unclean.	I *have an expectation* that the cleaners *should* always do a thorough job.

The point is that it is not the event but your expectation regarding that event that is the source of stress. You upset yourself since you own the expectation. The issue is who is upsetting whom? See yourself not *as* upset but rather as *having* an unmet expectation. Then decide if it is reasonable or not.

Changing from *being* upset to *having an unmet expectation* tells it like it is. It is a little like the difference between *having* a coat on and *being* that coat. Making this distinction puts a space between your person and your expectation-upset. You can choose to keep the "expectation-coat" on or you can drop it off. Perhaps you are beginning to capture that the whole upset business is your choice.

Of course, nowhere is it written that life or others *should* always come through for us, that life and others *should* always meet our needs. It is the Controller-Demander or Child-in-us that expects the unreal.

We can literally use anxiety, pain and anger then as tools to get a handle on what our expectations are.

Expectations: demands vs. attitudes

We need to be careful here. After reading this, you may decide, "OK, the way to avoid upsetting myself is not to expect anything of me or anyone else." This cynical attitude is not being advocated nor is it Nurturing.

Besides, what about the self-fulfilling prophecy that we tend to live up to our own and others' expectations? If you expect to do well at something, you are more likely to. If you expect others to co-operate they are more apt to. If you expect to fail, you make it more likely that you will. There are ample data showing that the self-fulfilling prophecy does operate.

This seeming discrepancy rests on the fact that there are two kinds of expectations. And it is important to make a distinction between the two.

There is one set of expectations experienced as "something due me." These "due me" expectations come from either the Child's *needs* or the Criticizer's *demands*. We'll look at a few of these in detail in the next chapter.

There is another kind of expectation. It springs not from need-demands but rather from an *attitude* toward ourselves or others. It is born of our faith or lack of it—a positive or negative belief in ourselves or others. A supportive, Nurturing attitude-expectation would be expressed as, "I believe Mary will remember the rules." On the other hand a Critical Parent attitude-expectation would be expressed as, "I know I can't ever count on Mary to co-operate."

We need to avoid confusing *need/demand-expectations* with *attitude-expectations*.

In checking your expectations list, the pain-producers will be the "due me" ones and those born of lack of faith. Be aware that "due me" expectations block faith in the other. You are freer to have positive attitudes toward others when you are not on the "You owe it to me" tape.

Let's look at how to change pain-producing expectations.

Need vs. want

A basic and almost universal expectation causing pain occurs when

I "want" or "prefer"
becomes
I "need";
the unfilled claim
becomes pain.

The Dependent Child-in-us still thinks in terms of survival-needs-that-only-parents-can-meet. As a child it probably was your "just due" to have those needs met.

As an adult, however, most of your needs are now within your power to fill through effort on your part. But if your Inner Child is given center stage you feel and act as if your wants, wishes, preferences are still dire needs that only others can satisfy. You automatically choose to put yourself in a dependent position when you feel others "owe" you. Laying these claims on your mate, friends, children, you feel as if your world will end should others not come through for you.

Helen, for example, felt she *needed* others to take the initiative. Always waiting for others to extend invitations, she was painfully lonely much of the time. She removed that pain when she switched her thinking to, "I *want* others to call me because I'm not used to making the effort and running the risk of refusal. But I'd rather take a chance than be this lonely."

Bob looked at his *need* for the status-giving promotion that didn't materialize. When he changed his thinking from need to preference, his devastated feelings lessened remarkably.

"Sure," he said, "I wanted the recognition that job brings. But I'm not going to drop dead without it and I do like my present setup. I'm going to get active with the 'hot line' volunteers. There's a place where my wish to make a difference can really be satisfied."

Write out your personal list of "I need's" for each significant person and situation in your life. Is each one a genuine need—something you *must* have to survive? Or is it a "prefer" or "want"—something you would like but won't drop dead without?

Needs serve a purpose. Obviously some are realistically legitimate. Others are not. Too often by thinking you need from another you can avoid providing for yourself. Such a claim shifts the responsibility once again from self to others. It allows you to hold on to the Child's illusion of being dependent. And victimized if the need goes unfilled. The payoff, as always, is the avoidance of self-responsibility.

Needs come from lacks or deficiencies. What are the lacks behind the needs on your list?

"I need you to be protective" might more truly be stated as "I lack the confidence to stand up for myself," "I don't want to have to exert myself—you do it for me," or "When I was a child I lacked someone to stick up for me and I still see myself as the Helpless Child needing an outside protector."

Ask yourself these questions:

What is it I want that I am not getting?

Which "I" in me wants it? This is a problem to which of my tapes?

What is the expectation of that "I"? Is it my Child or Criticizer demanding its "just due"?

Is it a need or a prefer?

From whom do I want it?

Are they the only ones who can help me get it?

"I *need* to talk about my feelings but my sister pulls back from feeling talk," fumes Barbara. She gives up her frustration by saying, "I wish she would join me in feeling talk. But she won't so I'll talk to someone who will." Now Barbara assumes the responsibility for meeting her own preferences. And she doesn't keep banging on the person who doesn't have what she'd like.

So often we ask a few people—usually one or two—to meet all our "prefer's-experienced-as-needs." Many of us ask our mate or a loved one to be the sole "filler" of our emotional buckets. It's too much to ask of one person. An impossible demand.

Dependent adults feature their Child tape that demands and expects others to meet their "want's-experienced-as-needs." They run around looking for a Giant Mother-Father Angel who never criticizes, who always gives. You can see how unrealistic such an expectation search is. Such people do not separate needs from "want's" or "prefer's." They do not choose to get what they want themselves. They sit—waiting for others to provide. They refuse to nurture themselves.

By switching what formerly were true needs from childhood to Adult preferences, you automatically give up the Demanding, Helpless Child stance. This shift from Child dependency needs is central to growing free. Only when we tend to our Needy Inner Child with our Inner Nurturer and Adult do we truly begin appreciating others in an affirming way.

Tight or loose

Expectations born of needs are clutched tightly. When you change them to "prefer's" you hold them lightly. This allows you to live life more flexibly, to roll with the punches. There's a whale of a difference in how you experience life when you make this shift.

Probably all of us have at least a few need/demand-expectations that are important to us in maintaining our integrity. We don't want to commit ourselves to or invest in an ongoing relationship unless they are fulfilled. On those points we are non-negotiable. Just a few are not likely to get in your way. But when you experience pain in a relationship, check for unrealistic hang-over Child-needs and Criticizer-demands. Both are attempts at control.

Self-accepting adults know the difference between their few basic needs and their many preferences. They are Nurturing Parents to themselves. Consequently, they do not set up dependent sucking relationships. They do not use their needs to knead themselves and others into Helpless Victims.

You haven't released life, others or yourself until you untie the straightjacket of unrealistic needs/demands.

Release comes
before acceptance.

Love only blooms when we accept what is. Controlling others and loving them are not in the same ball park. Clutching at others to fulfill our needs usually only drives them away. Or it produces never-ending struggles.

Release, let go and enjoy. That's the song of life. Live with preferences and then disappointments are few. With few disappointments you wear the garment of life loosely. With few unrealistic demands you wear the garment of life lovingly.

Now let's look at additional expectations that cause pain.

SEVEN

OTHER PAINFUL EXPECTATIONS

What's wrong vs. what's right

Do you appreciate yourself enough? Or do you dismiss the six pluses to wallow in the two minuses?

"Look for what's wrong and you will surely find it," said Abraham Lincoln.

How true this is. The imperfections in ourselves, others and life mean we can always find deficits if we try. Your Criticizer, of course, expects lacks and searches for defects relentlessly. Why not? The Criticizer has a vested interest in remaining active. To justify its existence, it needs grist for its mill. Otherwise it would have to close shop or at least step out of the limelight. To stay as a functioning part in your personality it must focus on what's missing. It grabs a magnifying glass to ferret out flaws. It cannot afford the looking glass that views the whole—both assets and liabilities.

Strengths, assets and "well done's" are taken for granted by the Criticizer. To see what's right would lessen the "Awful Me." Focusing on positives strongly enough sounds the death knell to Not-OKness. "Heaven forbid!" cries your Inner Criticizer.

Flip Wilson's "What you see is what you get" carries a potent

warning. Seeing only what's wrong with you gives your Not-OK
Child a gourmet dinner of guilt and shame. Conversely, rigorous
focus on what's right makes your self-esteem rise because Not-
OKness withers without negative inputs.

To get a quick reading on where your focus is, list all your shortcomings—the things you don't like about yourself. Then list all your
strengths—the things you do like about yourself.

In making your lists see if you used a double standard. That is,
did you list as weaknesses those things that are *occasionally* true
about you? On the other hand, in listing strengths did you insist
that such qualities *almost always* be true? If so, you stack the cards
against yourself—a typical Critical Parent trick.

Avoid this pitfall by reworking your lists. Make one "Occasional
strengths and shortcomings" and the other "Consistent strengths and
shortcomings."

Which list is longer? If liabilities outnumber strengths you are
Critical Parenting yourself. What is it that keeps your eyes riveted
on the negatives? Blind following of the "taught." You're "on automatic." You can choose to refocus, to reposition your viewpoint.

Self-nurturing means a commitment to self-compassion . . . a
positive attitude toward yourself. It means releasing old tapes that
focused on your lacks. You don't sweep your shortcomings under
the rug, but you persistently see the positives. Amazingly, the
"wrongs" carry less weight. What you expect is what you get. The
more you recognize your inner gold, the more it will shine and illu-
minate other previously unseen gold.

Lawbreakers are given sentences of a particular length. Once
their sentence is served, they're released. Do you dole out separate
life sentences for every flaw? Tell yourself you've spent years playing this game. Isn't it time you cried "Enough?" What's right de
serves equal time now.

Each right is a diamond; each wrong is a rock. Which do you
carry? Diamonds or rocks?

To be your own Nurturing Parent, expect to

**Look for
your stars,
not your scars.**

Refuse to be your own Rejecting Parent. It is an attitudinal expectation that causes untold pain.

Strength bombardment

If you earnestly want to increase your self-worth, here is a simple exercise that can help.

Throw out your earlier list of shortcomings. Ask a friend who knows you to see if he or she can add to your strengths list.

Each night before you go to bed and again on rising, stand in front of a mirror, list in hand. Look at your face and talk directly to yourself. Say "I like ————," putting the first positive in the blank. Pause and give yourself permission to feel the joy of possessing that quality. Go down the list repeating the procedure. When you've finished, smile warmly at yourself, pat your cheeks and say, "I *like* you."

Sound ridiculous?

How many times have you looked in the mirror and thought or said, "You creep," "You're awful," "Yuk!" or "I don't like you"? Why is it all right to clock hundreds of thousands of hours in disrespectful self-talk but not all right to give yourself a verbal pat? What satisfaction will come when on your deathbed you can say, "I've browbeaten myself for seventy-six (or ninety-nine) years?

If you believe in fair play at all, you believe in taking turns. Parole yourself from *concentrating only* on your shortcomings. Serve an eviction notice on that old Criticizer. You owe a debt to the long-silenced Nurturer in you.

Strength bombardment has nothing to do with conceit. It is a quiet, private time for welcoming your gifts. And it is only as you embrace your own that you can truly affirm the strengths in others. So what looks like self-puffing is only a necessary prelude to building up others, to focusing on what's right in them.

Chances are you will feel wiggly, awkward and maybe a bit foolish with this exercise. This only shows how thoroughly we are brainwashed to stay with the Criticizer rather than the Affirmer.

Consciously imagine this next week that you wear special glasses. They give you permission to see what's right with you. They do not ignore the minuses but they pull the pluses forward.

Consistently give yourself private support-talk just as a Nurturing Parent would:

Hey, look how you handled that! (*Joyfully*)
I'm excited about this triumph! (*No matter how small*)
I have faith in you; I believe you can!

One morning I dropped by a friend's house for a brief visit. She opened the door and greeted me with an enthusiastic, "Hi, Dorothy! Do come in. I just did fifteen minutes of the best mothering I've ever done. And I want to share this with you."

I almost dropped my skin!

There wasn't the least flavor of conceit or immodesty in what she said. There was simply a basic gladness and recognition she gave herself. What a refreshing contrast to the usual, "Let me tell you how terribly I've done!"

What about you? Do you ever greet your mate or a close friend with your gladnesses? Or only with your sadnesses? Do you give yourself permission to relish even the briefest of triumphs? If so, your Nurturer is on.

Strokes (little units of recognition) for *doing* feel great, of course. But the greatest stroke is the one for simply being—simply existing. When others give you this kind of stroke, it is pure gold. Perhaps you'll be better able to give yourself this golden Being-stroke after you've read the last chapter. That is the ultimate stroke we all need to work on giving to ourselves and others.

Loving, approving, accepting, reassuring, interested self-talk is what you need bushels of. Revel in delighted gladness about you. When you do this, you have your Inner Nurturer turned on.

From birth to death we all need strokes. Chronic stroke hunger makes you feel loveless. But privately given self-strokes remove us from the waiting-for-handouts line. Self-approval keeps us from manipulating others to give us the recognition we often refuse to give ourselves.

Absorbing the positives

Once your self-stroking campaign is under way, see if you don't notice a marked increase in the joy of being You. Gladness only comes, however, when you let each stroke in. Giving yourself approval is not enough. *Absorbing it is essential.* If you find this hard, you may be sure that your Not-OK Child has moved center front again. Its existence, remember, is based on not letting positives in. You can gently yet firmly set that Child aside.

If your self-esteem is low or shaky, you'll find self-stroking a most difficult exercise. Remember, your earlier programmed Belief System taught you to see only the negatives. You will now be going directly counter to the taped Critical View. And the Inner Criticizer will put up a mighty fuss should you look through any save its eyes. Just for fun, why not try disobeying? See the gold in you.

Take one of your pluses and at intervals throughout the day repeat this positive to yourself. Hug it close and enjoy basking in that private knowing. Give yourself permission to feel good about yourself.

If you only read through these exercises but choose not to do them, get with what is between you and doing them. Invariably it will be the Not-OK or Critical tapes that fight to keep the old status quo—pain.

Going my way

Rationally you may not think you hook into the expectation "Things *should* go my way." But check your upsets as was suggested earlier. They're born of this Child attitude. You may say with your mouth, "Oh well, you win some, you lose some." But what do your innards say?

When your body tirades or pouts or hurts if your "prefer's" don't materialize, inner peace is a mirage. You need to check your "due me" expectations.

Match mine

The upsets resulting from the Criticizer's expectation that "Others *should* value what I do" are rampant. It doesn't matter what the value is: promptness, order, rapid advancement, saving money, working hard, religion, politics, the status quo, security, new ideas, eating health foods, a slow or fast pace, fair play, a particular life-style.

Another way of experiencing this troublemaker is "Others *should* play by the same rules I do," or "Others *should* be like me."

Bud was furious with his wife's continual failure to keep commitments when they weren't convenient for her.

"She's done this again. I've put up with this for fifteen years in our marriage," he fumed. "And I bend over backward to keep *my* commitments! She makes my blood boil."

Beneath his rage was the belief that their values should match, that she should play by the rules he held to himself. Surely we can all understand his having upset feelings. But to continue to expect something after fifteen years of evidence to the contrary, however, is to be glued to non-reality. His wife didn't make his blood boil. Stubbornly holding on to his unrealistic expectation did.

The constant cry of the low self-esteemer or self-doubter is "Match me." He needs his position rubber-stamped. Difference is intolerable.

What is your attitude toward differences? Your answer is a clue to whether this "due me" expectation operates in you.

High self-esteemers give others space for difference. They avoid expectations that fly in the face of evidence to the contrary.

Once you get used to others' inability to be your match, you are more likely to enjoy them for where they are.

Ahead or behind

Comparing yourself to another is totally irrelevant, as will be most obvious after you've read the last chapter. But an extremely common expectation is "I *should* be better than others in all respects." Focusing on what he doesn't have, the loser gets his usual payoff in pain. Winners accept that in some areas they don't have it; in others they do. But they don't waste time comparing nor are they jealous of others who have more.

If your Not-OK Kid wants ammunition to feel "bad," it has no trouble finding someone who's further along in some skill, has more of some quality or advantage. If you want pain, you keep your eyes

on those who have more. You studiously avoid looking at those who
have less. Whom are *you* comparing yourself with?

Comparisons are so pervasive in homes, schools, sports and the
workaday world that it takes effort not to contaminate your focus.

Cultural attitudes fairly seem to shriek, "If yours is bigger you
have more value."

And we go after the big house, car, bank account, possessions,
trips, degrees, achievements, status. Society seems to say that size
and quantity prove the point. How much do you let these cultural
expectations serve as your personal guidelines?

Any time you find yourself feeling low because you think of someone who has more, consciously switch your thought to someone who
has less.

A basic truth is that

Gratitudes
and
unhappiness
do not co-exist.

Next time you feel down, stop and list all your gratitudes. Linger
over each one to savor the pure gladness of it. Your "down" is
most likely to change to an "up" at least temporarily. Leave nothing out of this list. Feel the gratitude of being alive; feel the gratitude of your body and all its miraculous parts. Relish the pleasure
of food and sex and sleep. List the marvels of your many learnings
—language, driving, reading and more. Think of those less fortu-
nate. Recall the advantages you have over people a hundred years
ago or in more disadvantaged spots in the world today. The simple
acts of walking, hearing and seeing are denied many less endowed
than you.

If you really try you could probably fill a book with gratitudes
galore. The pessimist complains of the noise when opportunity
knocks. The optimist sees the half-full glass, not the half-empty one.
What is the payoff when you fail to take time to be grateful? Pain
for that little Child-in-you.

What is your expectation? To have, to be the most? Or even 75
per cent in all departments? Or to enjoy the blessings that are al-

ready yours? He who keeps his eye on what he doesn't have never gets enough. She who relishes what she does have avoids making a career of deprivation. An attitude of gratitude is a priceless possession.

Plastic rose gardens

"Life and relationships *should* be plastic rose gardens." Who expects this? Most of us. Actually life is like a real rose garden. If you've raised roses you know that along with exquisite blooms come sharp thorns, aphids, weeds and a lot of work, time and care. Stunning blossoms rarely come spontaneously.

Life is a package deal. You keep your Not-OK Kid happy-in-its-unhappiness by expecting only sunny days, by always expecting the world to treat you fairly, justice always to prevail, happiness to descend without work on your part, all your ideals to come true, losses not to occur. The list of "due me's" is endless. Expecting lovely blossoms without time, care, effort and even pain is fantasyland. How much is your attitude toward life grounded in reality?

Look at the number of people who might say, "I know all that," and yet they prefer to anesthetize their pain rather than work through its source. Compulsive addictions of any kind (work, food, alcohol, gambling, pleasing) are ways to avoid facing pain. They temporarily deaden pain but they wipe out the joys of wholeness. The lovely blossom of wholehearted self-affirmation means not copping out through anesthesia. A deadened existence is not the goal of the high self-esteemer.

Crystal-ball gazers

"Life and others should anticipate my needs and be ready to meet them." It's easy for our Adult to dismiss this expectation. But check it out.

Far too many of us have the attitude that others should be crystal-ball gazers and we get out of joint when they're not. Pre-school children believe in magical thinking. They see their parents as clairvoyant. As adults we need to watch that we don't lay the magic trip on others.

Do you ask for what you want? Do you let it be known?

"Well," says Jeanie, "if I have to tell my husband what I want it subtracts from the joy of getting it." If you agree with this frequently expressed attitude, you hold to the Child-expectation that the other should be clairvoyant as to what you'd like.

"I tell my wife what I want but she doesn't come through," complains Ted. OK. Ask yourself, "Where is it written that others should give me what I want when I want it?" That's strictly Child tape. Surely it's nice if they do. But, once again, ask yourself if you'll expire if they don't. The depth of your disappointment is a clue to the intensity of your expectation.

If you don't ask for what you'd like, you reduce the chance of getting it. If you do ask, there's a chance you will receive but not a guarantee.

We need to watch that we don't rely on the tricky Deprived Child to choose whom we ask and what we ask for. It inevitably pushes us to ask for more than others can give. Or it reads deprivation into what is given. Or it pushes us to ask those who will reject. One way or another it tries to influence the outcome so that we don't receive. Remember,

**To wait for someone to
do something for you
contributes to the lessening of
your own self-esteem.**

The payoff for collecting disappointment stamps by expecting clairvoyancy is that it justifies not getting close. And the Not-OK Child as we know fears intimacy as well as responsibility.

Resistance

The pain from unrealistic expectations comes basically from resisting what is.

You want something and it isn't forthcoming. You resist asking for what you want. You resist its not coming your way.

You want others to buy your viewpoint or values but they don't.

You resist their non-acceptance. And twist it into rejection of your person rather than your viewpoint.

You cannot change the other or the outer. And you resist this reality.

Another rejects you, a loved one leaves, another gets or has more than you. The pain comes from resisting the facts.

To release the pain, release your resistance . . . let go . . . *let it be*.

Trigger events

From time to time we all overreact. But even when we know our response is out of proportion we're often in the dark as to why.

Sometimes, of course, overreactions come from letting a lot of little annoyances build up. It's fairly easy to avoid this Vesuvius by deciding to deal with the minor as it occurs. But what about the overreaction when such isn't the case?

Almost without exception you may be sure that the present event has touched a tender spot—*an undealt-with pain from your past*. The trigger event is but the tip of the iceberg.

Seen this way,

Overreactions can be used
as friends to pinpoint
the past source.

At this point you seemingly have two choices. Either deal with the past pain directly or avoid it. Most prefer the second alternative. We shy away from it. "Let sleeping dogs lie" is the usual attitude. But then the past pain deals with you indirectly . . . it lies in wait to resurface every time your tender spot is touched. Or to crop out in some symptom.

Actually you have only one choice if you want to be free. Past pains need to be dealt with directly if they are to be laid to rest permanently. Band-Aiding abscesses doesn't remove infected materials.

The factor giving this earlier pain its intensity and power is that it was *originally experienced by your Inner Child as a threat to its survival.* And around that first threat is an *accumulation of un-dealt-with feelings.*

Let's see how this dynamic worked in Mary's case. And how she freed herself by facing into the original pain and releasing those earlier unexpressed feelings.

Mary fumed violently when her friend Bea treated her unfairly. Impulsively she wanted to dish out a double dose of the same. But her Adult estimated the probable outcome of acting on that impulse. Experience told her tit for tat was non-productive.

So she wrote a scathing, strictly Critical Parent letter and then burned it. Next she got muscle relief by vigorously beating her rubber dishwashing gloves against the kitchen counter.

Psychological relief came with her awareness that Bea's unfairness only triggered a past rage toward her deceased father's unfairness to her as a child. Consciously moving her Helpless Child to center stage, she put into words the full force of all her feelings toward her father's treatment as if she were talking directly to him.

The unexpressed pent-up feelings and old pain were re-experienced and fully expressed. Empathically hearing her own Distressed Child—the great solvent for its pain—allowed her Adult to come forward. Gradually she realized her father had been unable to give what she needed. When her inner storm subsided, she vividly pictured releasing her Child-need-of-him. She imagined reaching out her Adult hand of understanding. She released him finally by imagining him standing in a stream enjoying an afternoon of fishing (his favorite sport). Having settled her unfinished business with him, a new kind of peace flooded in.

How did she handle Bea's unfairness? "It seemed so easy," said Mary. "I just told her that I really didn't like what she did. But I didn't have any need for a stormy overreaction."

Mary was aware that an expectation she put on Bea (as well as all others) was "Don't ever be unfair to me because I lived with unfairness for years." This expectation-demand was an attempt to keep the old "helpless-against-Daddy's-unfairness" feelings repressed. When she was unable to control others' unfairness, the Burned Child in her became enraged. The earlier unresolved pain was activated.

In working through her overreaction to Bea's treatment, Mary did not deny to herself her urge to retaliate. She didn't tell herself she was "bad" (Critical Voice) for wanting to get even. Yet, she didn't act out (Impulsive Child) on Bea. She gave her Critical Parent's urge to lash out and her Child's need to weep a safe place for expression. No harm came to anyone from this method of handling her reaction.

You can easily imagine that in light of her past experience with unfairness it was a loaded area for Mary. It triggered old pain. It is easy to see that just as she reacted violently to Bea's treatment, she would want to do the same to herself if she ever felt she was unfair. Her expectation, her emotional demand born of past pain, was "unfairness is out." Yet, realistically there will be times when she and others will not be fair. It is unrealistic—an impossible ideal—to expect unfairness not to occur from time to time.

Working through tender spots

All of us have some tender spots—undealt-with pain from the past. And from time to time some person or event in our present pushes that button. *Then we react to the present situation with the full force of the undealt-with past pain.* Our innards react as if our very survival is threatened.

How can you constructively defuse old tender spots?

You use the same basic formula with yourself that nurturing parents follow to free their children of negative emotions. *You empathically encourage the expression of those feelings in a safe place.*

Before looking at the steps of the process, an important caution needs to be sounded. Just as nurturing parents help their children work through the ordinary negative feelings that occur in the child's day, they turn to professionals when serious emotional symptoms exist. Do not try to treat yourself if you have noticeable emotional discomfort or symptoms. You know you might take an aspirin for an occasional headache, but you see a doctor if the headache persists or if you feel basically under par.

Similarly, working through major emotional pains is to be done with a well-trained professional who can provide the guidance, safety and support your Hurting Child needs. He or she gives you the necessary corrective emotional experience. The minor discomforts you can handle yourself. One fact is clear: excessive unfinished business with the past stands between relating to yourself and others freely in the present.

The process for working out tender spots is:

1. See the present trigger even as an opportunity to flush out old festered material so that you are free of it once and for all.

2. As stage director of your inner drama, give conscious permission for your Criticizer or Pained Child to express its feelings. (The Nurturing Parent understands that negative feelings disappear when they are released in a safe place.) For some of you the Attacker Voice may be uppermost in your awareness. For others the Devastated Abandoned One may be closest to the surface. Regardless, move your Blame or Pain Voice to center stage. *But choose the time and place and vehicle for airing and acting out these feelings toward the trigger event so that no harm comes to you, others or property of value.*

3. Once you've dealt with the present person or situation, ask yourself, "Who from my childhood, or what event in those days, triggered similar reactions in me?" Now imagine that earlier person with you—or the earlier event as presently occurring. Move into your Hurt, Pleading, Helpless, Rebellious Child or the Blaming, Punishing, Judgmental Criticizer. Express all the feelings now that you didn't dare reveal originally. Leave nothing unexpressed.

Sometimes using a single word or phrase like "No," "Stop," "Help," "Please," "Give me," "I'll control you," "Don't," and so on is helpful. If your volume might disturb others, use a pillow over your mouth to deaden the sound. Stay with each feeling until it is spent.

If words don't suffice, let out the sound that expresses the feelings. Some of our deepest feelings are wordless. With each exhalation let your breath carry the tone. Your voice belongs to your body, not to your head. Let it speak (cry, rage) out.

If you're dealing with anger, express it with words, tones and physically. Intense feelings disappear most completely when they are acted out. A batacca, pillow, punching bag, mattress, clay or paint can provide the needed outlets.

When anger is spent, almost invariably a helpless, powerless feeling eventually surfaces. Why? Because *anger is a second feeling*—a cover-up for a more primary emotion. That first feeling may be hurt, frustration, fatigue, deprivation, shock, disappointment, worry, fear, rejection, embarrassment, failure or any other. Each can reactivate old Helpless Child feelings. And convert to anger or rage.

Helplessness and aloneness seem to be *the* Child feelings we most shy away from re-experiencing. You may be strongly tempted to avoid allowing them into awareness. Remind yourself that repressed emotions always have the last word. Give yourself permission to have done with them so that they do not splash out on unsuspecting targets or against yourself.

You've heard that children need quality time with their parents. What you are doing here is giving quality time—totally focused, unhurried, non-judgmental time—to the little Child feelings that needed someone to hear so long ago. Let your Inner Nurturer stand by to accept all those pent-up emotions.

Feelings have power and energy. Your emotions gear you for fight or flight. In jungle days they had survival value and there's no way you can order them around. Emotional and physical survival depend on recognizing this fact. Whenever you try to command feelings you do so at great cost to yourself and others. As the ad says, "You can't fool Mother Nature." Your body always knows when you try to.

4. Once the feelings are finished—you'll recognize that stage by a kind of cleaned-out feeling—mentally imagine picking up your Little Child. Rock it gently in your arms; comfort it; say the words it so needed to hear long ago. Reassure it that you (Inner Nurturer) stand by to meet its needs, to protect it, to love it unconditionally.

5. The next step involves positive imaging. If it was an event that caused pain imagine the event reoccurring but this time without pain to you. If it was a person that caused pain because of something he or she did or did not do or say, vividly restructure the scene with a positive outcome. See yourself as free of that person or situation. Let the other float away in your imagination. See yourself as separate and no longer needing or hurting. Release and forgive.

Until you release the other, you are tied to that person in a negative way. Until you release, you are not free.

6. Even when much of the old pain has been worked through, you'll doubtless continue to run into trigger events for those old tender spots. But now you know that event "X" from today only touches off event "A" from your childhood. And you can choose to remind yourself (with your Adult) that this present person or event is not the original one.

7. Finally, get involved in some task that requires an outward focus—gardening, reading, sewing, polishing your car.

Hearing out past pains in a safe place (with a trained professional if pain is strong), discharging unexpressed feelings appropriately and nurturing your Inner Deprived Child gives you control over your personal drama. Positive picturing and giving your Adult a job help rebalance your focus.

Said Pat, "I still get hot when I see other women getting any kind of recognition instead of me. But I remind myself that as a kid I was jealous that my three sisters made it with my mom while I didn't. That really hurt; it's my tender spot. Now that I've worked through that hurt, I remind myself that the recognition-giver is not my mother and these other women are not my sisters. I'm able to figure out what's going on in me and kind of laugh at how easy it is for my Rejected Kid to bounce up front in these situations. And now I tell that little Kid that I'll never reject her and I give her a strong dose of what's right about her. Then I find something fun or challenging to work on. It really has helped me no end."

Positive thinking

How does positive thinking fit in with permitting yourself to express negatives?

When you know who the Real You is, your thinking about yourself cannot be anything but positive, as we'll see later.

But for many who use it, positive thinking does not last. It has to be constantly reapplied. Why? Because you're applying it on top of negative feelings born of past pains. That is like putting fresh paint over rust. It constantly peels off.

If you feel sad but tell yourself you are happy, you need to apply "happy" paint repeatedly. The underlying sadness keeps eating away the surface happiness. The rule is to let the pain out first and then move to positive imaging.

Safely expressing negatives then gets the rust off. Almost automatically the positives will flow in. If they don't, we'll show you how later through the process of positive mental picturing. Then the positive knowing remains because the rust of the negatives is gone.

Caution

Because we usually read while in our Adult tape, some of the pain-producing expectations discussed here may not seem to fit for you at first. But check your behavior; check your reactions. They come off inner expectations. Watch for trigger events. With careful observation you can gradually pull hidden expectations and past hurts to the surface. Awareness of how you use expectations and unfinished business to upset yourself gives you the power to choose other alternatives—the power to get off automatic—the power to live with far greater freedom.

Piercing the wall of past conditioning is not always easy. But the old destructive ways need to go if you want to increase your self-esteem, if you want to live fully.

Awareness, as always, is the first step. The second necessary one is the courage to give up the old, the known. Courage to risk the new. Safe action is the final step that gets the process under way.

Now let's look at the third and strongest pain-maker, judgment, to see how to free yourself from its clutches.

EIGHT

JUDGMENT: THE DANCE OF DEATH

The three culprits

"Should's" give rise to expectations and vice versa. These two till the soil for self-blame when you don't measure up. The three—garden-variety "should's," unreasonable expectations and self-judgments—are welded together like the prongs of a pitchfork. They make up the powerful tool for inflicting self-pain.

If your self-esteem is low, you may be sure you stab yourself relentlessly with these prongs. Self-blame lies at your core. The very statement "I'm not lovable; I don't count" is a negative self-judgment. As we've seen, it forms the heart of your negative self-image.

The major weapon of the Critical Parent is defused when you halt the blame game. Yet, if you are a self-hater or doubter, you play it continually.

Self-discounts

How often do you hear yourself say or think:

I forgot to pick up the laundry; *what a klutz!*
I really put my foot in that one. *How could I be so stupid?*

I left the car lights on—*Dunce! Will you never learn?*
How terrible of me to have thought about not going!

Sound familiar? Your Critical Voice is on. And each such
thought—each such statement—is anti-love. These litanies are daily
fare for far too many of us. Check yourself here. Write out your
own private list—those statements you make about something
you've done, said, or felt and the ensuing judgment. In each case it
is the second step—the judgmental blast—that feeds your Not-OK
Child. Self-put-downs keep it fat and powerful.

Positive labels

Even benign self-judgments keep you living with a judge on your
back.

> I gave to the Red Cross; *I'm a good citizen.*
> I handled that situation constructively; *I'm a competent
>   manager.*
> I stayed on my diet; *I'm a good girl.*

Judgment, benign or critical, keeps self-worth tied to acts,
thoughts, feelings. When you play judge, your OKness is always
conditional. Such an "if-then" relationship within never allows you
to develop a solid sense of self-esteem. Your worth is forever on a
scale balanced against your judgment of your performance. Remember,

Pain is the name
of the game
between the Critical Parent and Not-OK Child.

There is no better way to ensure pain than self-blame. Each of us
reaps what we sow. Judgments are seeds that bring only a harvest of
trouble. They pollute our inner world. Your emotional well-being
depends directly on freeing your Child from judgmental verdicts.
No more potent poison to inner peace and contentment exists.

Reaction vs. judgment

What is the answer to ridding yourself of this poison? The answer is simple:

**React
but do not
judge.**

Let's go back to our earlier statement. Let's drop off the judgment and substitute a personal reaction to the event.

I forgot to pick up the laundry; *I sure wish I hadn't.*

I really put my foot in that one. *Next time I'll handle it this way.*

I left the car lights on; *what an inconvenience!*

I thought about not going but that would really disappoint the others. And *I don't choose to do that.*

I gave to the Red Cross; *I'm glad I did.*

I handled that fight constructively; *I'm happy about that.*

I stayed on my diet; *I'm pleased with that choice.*

Now in each situation you *react* to your behavior; you do not insult your person. Nor do you tie your self-worth to your behavior.

Person vs. behavior

The basic idea here—and it is a crucial one—is to

**Separate your person
from
your behavior, thoughts, feelings.**

Every low and shaky self-esteemer lives with the basic belief: "I am what I do." (Remember this is what the Criticizer teaches, while the Nurturer teaches that you are separate from your behavior.)

As long as you believe that you are what you do, you live a yo-yo-like existence. You truly perform a dance of death. You wipe out the possibility of inner peace. You keep yourself from believing you are lovable.

No one concept is more difficult to grasp. From our earliest moments most of us have been swamped with words and body language pounding home one lesson: *you are what you do.*

"Such a good baby" meant "Such convenient behavior."

"You are a good patient" meant "You behaved so that it was convenient to work with you."

"Be a good boy" meant "Clean your plate."

"You're a good class" meant "You followed the rules."

"You're a bad girl" meant "You pouted and I don't like pouting."

"You're rude" meant "You interrupted and I don't appreciate that behavior."

The list goes on ad nauseum.

Tens of thousands of times your *person* was assigned a badge of "good" or "bad" based on *how you behaved* or *thought* or *felt.* The most natural conclusion in the world then is "My worth, my OKness or Not-OKness, depends on my behavior, thoughts, feelings."

Let's face it. Your behavior may need changing, but *you* are not your behavior even though your acts come from you. For example, let's look at the sentence "You ran home." "You" is the subject, the doer, the actor. "Ran" is the behavior, the verb, the action. You know that nouns or pronouns are not verbs. They name the person; the verb tells about the act. You, the person, are not your running. Nor are *you* your crying, your stubbornness, your joy, your refusal, your anger, your patience. *The actor is not the action. The person is not the behavior.*

The actor may behave in acceptable or non-acceptable ways. But the behavior is separate from the person even though it *comes from* the person. Just as blood comes from you, it is not you. You take a giant step toward high self-esteem when you absolutely refuse to confuse the two. And *full-fledged self-acceptance does not come until you make this separation.*

A three-year-old started asking his mother repeatedly, "Mama, do you love me?" Each time she answered, "Of course I do." Then the child would take her hand, lead her to a broken flowerpot or shattered toy and look at her questioningly. The mother was confused about her toddler's repeated performance.

Here was a little child, on this earth only three short years, already asking one of the most profound psychological questions any of us can ask: "Is my lovability tied to what I do? Am *I* the same as my behavior?"

Unfortunately, most of us believe we are what we do. Living off this "if-then" blueprint, we must perform or our self-worth perishes.

The importance of this point cannot be overemphasized. To increase self-worth it is vital that you react to your behavior while remaining friendly toward your person. Each time you react rather than judge you are a Nurturing Parent to yourself. This new way of thinking and talking will be in direct contradiction to your Critical Parent blasts, of course.

Start today and make a game of watching for self-blame talk. Each time you slip, stop. Rephrase the sentence as a reaction. You might ask your family or a close friend to help you listen for those self-spanking words.

You may find yourself with a speech problem for a while but you'll soon be talking constructively to and about yourself.

The suicide note left by a sixteen-year-old boy read, "If I fail in what I do, I fail in what I am." "If-then" thinking causes death physically or psychologically; there is no escaping its toll. To continue such an inner uproar has only one payoff: it helps you keep sad/bad feelings, those familiar, known strokes.

When Self blame stops your Not-OK Child shrinks.

Remember, self-blame leads to blaming others, fate or the universe and subsequent attempts to control—to victimize or be victimized. No matter how you slice it, blame is a no-good trip. "Judge not" is an imperative with vital consequences.

Potty-training syndrome

Shifting from destructive to constructive self-talk will follow a pattern.

You decide to give up your shoulditis and judgment. Conviction and resolve. You're off on a new path. But in spite of your new awareness, you revert. You may be tempted to think or say, "Here I know about these pitfalls and yet I go right ahead and use them again. How could I be so dumb?" (Hear the self-judgment?)

None of us moves from A to Z in one leap. There is a sequence that all new learnings take. Think about potty training.

The little one has the basic idea. He comes to you and says, "Gotta go," and he stands there sopping. He tells you *after* the fact. But he has made progress. At least he comes to you and uses the words. Earlier in his training he didn't.

A few days later he comes saying he has to go and right as he tells you, the urine streams down. He tells you *during* the event.

Then comes the glorious day when he tells you *before* he goes. If you've potty-trained children, you expect this sequence.

So it will be with you. In spite of your new awareness and your best intentions, you will find yourself responding with the old habitual self-put-downs. Two minutes, two hours or two days later your new awareness will hit. *After* the event. At that moment you hold the choice as to how to react. You can choose to beat yourself with negative judgment because you *"should* have known better." Or you can applaud yourself that you are on step one—the *after* step.

Next, you will be aware right at the time of your shoulditis or self-judgment. But you will go ahead and let your Not-OK Child have it anyway. Congratulate yourself! You are on step two—the *during* step. You'll get to the third stage—the *before* step—in due time.

Your Nurturing Parent does not ask you for growth or change overnight. It is not a punishing Voice. It knows all about the potty-training syndrome. It has implicit faith that the sequence of after, during and before will unfold with continued effort. It judges not; it supports; it is patient with growth; it believes you can change.

Three myths

Part and parcel of the "if-then" trap you can fall into is believing three myths. Each involves a judgment.

> If I am pretty or handsome, I have more worth.
> If I am smart, I have more value than the less mentally gifted.
> If I get to the top, I am more worthy than if I don't.

Obviously there is not a great deal you can do about your basic physical endowment. Yet our culture places great stress on physical beauty. You men are likely to feel inadequate if you are short or less brawny. You women may envy the glamor girl with the svelte form.

The size and shape of the package—the whole form or only the nose—has nothing to do with your worth *unless* you buy this myth. And if your self-esteem is shaky, your Not-OK Child will look for ammunition against itself. Movies, TV and magazines give that destructive tape plenty of material if you choose to use it.

Yet surely you know the physically unattractive person whose features you rarely notice because you cherish his or her Inner Being. Studies show that physical attractiveness does not guarantee high self-esteem. Actually great beauty can be a real handicap; it can threaten others and may be relied on so that inner potentials go undeveloped. It tends to fade with age.

A fascinating thing happens when physically rather unattractive people increase their self-worth. They start making the most of their physical appearance; they dress more attractively; they choose more complimentary colors; they take better care of their bodies. So often as this change takes place, they say, "You know, I'm not so bad-looking after all." That's always music to the counselor's ears.

Intelligence as measured by present IQ tests is only a score giving an estimate of how the white middle-class person will probably handle mental abstractions. It is not an indicator of creativity, motivation or emotional stability. Remember, inner peace comes from how you relate to yourself and others, not solely through skill in manipulating abstractions.

Intellectual gifts are not to be put down; those who have them hopefully develop and use them. But they do not give the owner an automatic ticket to high self-worth. History is filled with geniuses whose brilliance wasn't enough.

Similarly, achievements brought about by the joy of working through a challenge or developing a skill are not to be scoffed at. It's fun and deeply satisfying to develop our talents, be they grand or small. But in and of themselves they won't give wholehearted self-acceptance. There are scores of people who have collected one triumph after another who remain miserably unhappy.

As with making the most of your physical assets, so with intelligence and achievements. Success in school, on the job and in activities is more likely when you feel self-respect and self-confident. Your energy goes outward to meet the challenges and is not wasted on inner turmoil.

Attractive, bright achievers have assets that can increase their joy in being themselves. But these assets can only be inwardly enjoyed when they are *added to* basic self-respect. Without that prime ingredient, inner peace eludes them. Every counselor can document this truth with hundreds of cases. Daily we see beautiful, skilled achievers with low self-esteem.

By the same token, there are physically unattractive persons with limited mentality and few achievements who thoroughly enjoy others and life. They accept their limitations, waste no energy on bewailing and focus on what they do have and can do. They do not buy "if-then" thinking. They are living proof that the trappings do not guarantee peace. We can all learn from them.

Judgment from others

"What good does it do to stop my self-judgments when others judge my person by my acts? I only fool myself if I think I am free of that."

Yes, unfortunately judgment from others is rampant and it is likely that many others will not separate your person from your behavior. However, the central issue is not whether another judges you, but rather whether you accept that judgment.

Suppose, for instance, that I lash out at you and say, "You're nothing but an opportunist!" You hear my judgment but in your heart you are completely confident that you are not and have never been an opportunist. That judgment simply does not fit. In all likelihood you'll figure my dander is up about something, but the gibe doesn't find its mark.

On the other hand, suppose I call you a "big phony." And let's imagine that much of the time you do pretend to be something you're not. You hear my judgment; it fits your own self-judgment and you absorb the hurt. We often say, "It is the truth that hurts."

Assume you have the habit of inwardly reacting to your behavior rather than judging your person. When I call you a "big phony" you do a quick inner translating job. You think, "Yes, sometimes I choose to put up a façade for whatever reason." But you do *not* inwardly add, "And that shows that I am an awful person."

You simply refuse to judge yourself.

In addition, you can choose to translate my judgment of your person into *my reaction* to your façade. Inwardly you think, "Dorothy would prefer that I not pretend to be something I'm not." In other words, you take my judgment and reword it. You turn it into *my reaction toward your behavior*. And you give me the right to own that reaction. You give me the space to judge if that's what I need to do. But you studiously avoid letting my need to judge control your inner self-talk.

You do not let others' judgments trigger your Self judgment.

You don't buy into the guilt trip others try to lay on you. You don't give them that power over you.

Basically then many others will judge your person. But you can choose whether you absorb that judgment as ammunition against your Inner Child. Or whether you turn the other's judgment into their reaction and give them the space to do their number.

Being your own Nurturing Parent means separating your person from your acts, thoughts and feelings. It means you react to them; you refuse to judge. Such a shift in your Belief System and self-talk sounds simple but it isn't.

Said Bob, "I'm awed that by these relatively simple changes in thinking about myself I somehow seem to feel so much more content with myself. But it is very hard to be consistent with it because I've lived so long with that other stuff going on in my head. I refuse, however, to stop working at breaking my old habits."

Once you choose to release the three prongs of "should's," unrealistic expectations and self-judgments, you are well on your way to high self-esteem. Those Not-OK feelings will decrease noticeably.

The next step is to free yourself from replaying your life scene as your early models did. This means challenging some of their injunctions and giving yourself some new permissions.

· NINE ·

COPIED OR FREE

Copied styles

Part of Self nurturing means prying free of negative modeling copied from the significant people in your past.

We humans are born imitators. We mimic the upright position, language, dress, attitudes and customs. Many of our positive imitations help us function well with ourselves and others. They are pro-life.

The pain-producing patterns we adopted, however, block us from embracing the joy of living. To do away with them we need first to know what they are.

Make a list of pro- and anti-life attitudes and styles you saw modeled in childhood. Note who modeled what. Your list might start this way:

PRO-LIFE:	ANTI-LIFE:
Enjoy learning (*mother*)	Don't learn (*father*)
Have fun (*father*)	Don't play (*mother*)
Be real (*father, mother*)	Don't be real (*older sister*)

Be optimistic (*father*)	Don't be optimistic; worry (*mother*)
Get involved (*sister, father*)	Don't get involved (*mother, brother*)
(No model for being realistically responsible)	Be overly responsible—to a fault (*mother, father*)
(No model for co-operating with or working under an authority figure)	Don't let others have any power over you (*mother, father*)
(No model that men are OK)	Men are basically no good (*mother, father, brother, sister*)
Co-operate but be true to convictions (*grandfather, sister*)	Rebel or give up (*sister, brother*)

Continue observing your daily interactions, attitudes and reactions. Add each new awareness to either side of your list. Ask yourself, "Who from my past had a similar attitude or style? Who in my past would have reacted as I just did?" Consciously look at your answers to these questions.

How did each of my significant others play life?

What was each one's attitude toward self? others? men? women? nature? work? play? sex? authority figures? helpless ones? learning? emotions?

Who played Criticizer? Victim? Rescuer? Peacemaker? Confronter? Distracter? People-pleaser? Dependable? Irresponsible? Undecided? Understanding? Responsible? Goof-off? Denier?

What roles were assigned in my family? Who held the power? Who made the decisions? How? Who played "Bad Guy"—the pain-bearer for the family? Who played "Good Guy"—who could do no wrong? Who played Pessimist? Optimist? Who played Official Worrier? Official Guilt-bearer? Who played Achiever? The family Status-collector? Who played Clown? Who played Cross? Who was the heavy? Who manipulated whom and how?

Who was ignored? Who got the attention (negative or positive)?

Who was scared most of the time? Who was happy?

How was crisis handled? Who fell apart? Who rose to the occasion?

Whose values predominated?

This list of questions is only partial. If you look carefully enough you'll find that each significant person in your life modeled certain life stances. And as children we often unthinkingly adopt and mimic their various attitudes, life positions, expectations and roles. Then, unless we choose otherwise we may blindly copy those others the rest of our lives without giving the matter a second thought.

Now ask yourself, "What role or stance is typical for me? How did I come to buy into this role? Did I copy it? Was it assigned to me? Was it my way of getting recognition? Was it my way of establishing an identity separate from those others?"

Really take time to think through these questions.

If you identified most strongly with one person in your childhood you may be reading off their lines exclusively. On the other hand, you may use your father's script except in times of crisis when you adopt your mother's lines. You may have brewed up your own pattern for handling work, used your older brother's for play, your mother's for marriage, your grandfather's for parenting. In short, some of us bought one model lock, stock and barrel. Others of us have a thirty-one-flavors blend.

The first task is to identify what was modeled for you.

The second task is to ask yourself, "What am I doing today, how am I relating, that is simply an imitation of what I saw lived out before me? Is it a pattern that is pro- or anti-life? What are the consequences if I continue it? Drop it? Whose life am I living? Mine or others'?"

For Nancy's mother martyrdom was a life-style. Unintentionally, Nancy copied her mother's script by blindly playing Grievance Collector. Nancy was "on automatic"—always playing Done-in. Without awareness of this she could easily live out her entire life reading her mother's life lines, never separating herself out to become her own person.

Paula found herself gloomy each morning even when things went well. She couldn't pinpoint the reason until she became aware that this was the familiar mood her parents modeled. She had given up her early spontaneous joy in facing a new day. She needed to ask herself, "What's in it for me to simply copy? Am I willing to write my own lines? To respond as me?"

On the other hand, rather than blind copying, some of us see a particular style modeled and blindly react by compulsively doing the opposite. Katherine's mother pessimistically complained and constantly found fault. Katherine was so turned off by her mother's attitude that she played compulsive Happy Face. She refused to give herself permission to have even a legitimate discontent about any situation. Katherine had to think or act Z wherever her mother would have thought or acted A. She denied herself the whole range of choices from B to Y.

You are just as unfree if your choose to play Completely Opposite as when you decide to play Total Copy. Neither choice allows you to trail blaze You.

Seek new models

If both your parents (or several significant others) consistently modeled one attitude, you were more heavily programmed in that direction. This is particularly so if it blends with your genetic makeup.

Ted's parents, for example, were both heavily into passive-dependency. From birth Ted had been of an easygoing nature. He did what came naturally—he copied their style. Neither his models nor his basic energy level gave him the push to change even though this lack of self-assertion characteristically meant he lost out. If he chose to be more assertive and less dependent, he would need to put forth more effort than if he had been born with more innate assertiveness or if even one of his parents had provided such a model.

How you choose to face life then is affected not only by your models and how many around you modeled the same approach, but also by your genetic makeup. If one parent modeled a pro-life attitude while the other modeled an anti-life one, it is easier to get on the pro-life side. You have at least experienced a close model to imitate. If both were negative, you need to work harder for change. *But this does not mean you cannot change.*

Actively seek pro-life models. Observe them closely. And tap into your human capacity to imitate. You know that if you want to learn a foreign language, you expose yourself to that language. And you start imitating. The process of modeling for positive life attitudes is the same. You are merely learning a new language called pro-life.

Injunctions vs. permissions

Important others from your childhood may not only have been anti-life models. They may have actively taught you to discount, dismiss or disown certain natural parts of yourself. These injunctions, housed in the Critical Parent, taught loser ways that block functioning as a whole person.

The more extensively and completely such injunctions rule your life, the less control you have over it. They cripple your effectiveness and your ability to love yourself and others. And they add to helpless, Not-OK feelings.

In contrast pro-life permissions come from the Nurturing tape. To increase your self-worth the spoken and unspoken anti-life injunctions ruling you need to be turned into appropriate permissions.

Common injunctions

Here is a partial list of all too common injunctions. Some of these may be in your programming; some may not be. Some you live with are unlisted. Spend time thinking about each one and add any of your own that are not mentioned.

As you go down the list you'll recognize certain injunctions as obviously part of your how-to-live-life blueprint. Check these first. Then spend some time watching how you respond to yourself, others and life to see if you can identify some of the less obvious ones.

Don't fail to produce constantly.

Don't produce at all.

Don't lose; Don't win.

Don't hang in and fight.

Don't forgive or forget.

Don't reach out to others.

Don't disagree; don't agree.

Don't explore or be curious.

Don't start anything new till you've finished what you've started.

Don't have fun or be playful.

Don't be lighthearted.

Don't be serious.

Don't confront.

Don't talk straight or level.

Don't be yourself.

Don't challenge or question an "authority."

Don't go along with any authority figure.

Don't ever get under obligation to others.

Don't be needy—hungry emotionally.

Don't get close.

Don't listen to your body wisdom, your intuition.

Don't assert yourself.

Don't use your ability.

Don't be smart.

Don't think for yourself.

Don't co-operate.

Don't be assertive.

Don't let go; don't fail to keep in control.

Don't make a mistake. Don't be wrong.

Don't stay calm in a crisis.

Don't fail to live up to others' expectations.

Don't be real.

Don't reveal yourself.

Don't see the humorous in life.

Don't like yourself.

Don't exert yourself.

Don't feel. (Positive or negative emotions)

Don't take care of yourself.

Don't be independent.

Don't grow or change.

Don't plan.

Don't ask for help.

Don't give yourself recognition.

Don't think ahead about the outcome of a possible choice.

Don't give recognition.	Don't accept recognition.
Don't be responsible to self or others.	Don't conform.
	Don't be different.
Don't be passive.	Don't care.

You may be tempted to skim over such a long list. Hopefully you'll resist such a temptation. The personal list you live with may be even lengthier.

Once you've tagged an anti-life injunction in your life, consciously challenge remaining wedded to a teaching that cuts into vibrant living. Ask yourself what price you have paid for following it. Do you seriously want to continue to pay that price? Give yourself permission to weed out the culprits. This permission is part of Self nurturing, part of increasing self-worth.

Following these hidden injunctions literally squeezes out parts of your Being. Each one asks that you mold your responses into particular, rigid, predetermined patterns. Do you see how they limit you in terms of flowing freely and appropriately? When we are whole we allow ourselves the full range of styles depending on what is appropriate.

Exaggerating injunction choice

To get a full-fledged feeling for how an injunction that rules your life can narrow your options, pick one that seems dominant for you and exaggerate it. Go all out. (It is wise to practice the exaggeration with family or friends, not at work for obvious reasons. Alert others as to what you are doing so they don't think you've flipped your lid.)

If the injunction "Don't start anything new until you've finished what you've started" controls your life, exaggerate it.

Spend an entire day making sure that you rigidly finish *every* activity before starting another. This will mean that if you are eating and the phone rings, you don't answer it. If you are reading a book, don't let yourself stop till you've finished it no matter how bored, fatigued or pressed by other things. If you are talking to one person and another speaks to you, don't respond until you've finished your visit with the first person. If you are house cleaning and an outstanding TV program comes on, continue cleaning. You immediately see how you box yourself in if you live exclusively off any one injunction.

Few of you are this rigidly tied to the "finish what you start" edict. But if a novel bores you, must you finish it? If an interesting opportunity arises, can you let go of your compulsion to finish a chore if it can be responsibly handled later? If your child or mate wants to chat, must dinner preparations take priority every time?

Exaggerating an injunction helps you see how any blind following asks you to put aside spontaneity, practicality, flexibility and listening to your inner wisdom. It serves to put a lid on your Nurturer, Adult and Natural Child.

Appropriate permissions

Before you lift off an injunction, check the appropriateness of canceling it. You do this by tuning in your Adult tape.

Giving yourself permission to "see the humorous" is probably inappropriate at most funerals. Giving up the injunction "Don't fail to live up to others' expectations" by staying home from work day after day can cost you your job. Really sharing your feelings with someone who is turned off by such is not in your best interest. Asking every Tom, Dick and Harry for recognition for everything you do obviously only pushes others away.

The rule is

Give yourself permissions
in appropriate situations.

Of course, if you are heavily programmed with injunctions, you may conclude that it is never appropriate to set them aside under most circumstances. Or if your Adult tape is weak, you may dump your injunctions inappropriately, run into negative feedback and then duck back under their protective cover. Professional help, personal growth classes or careful observation of those who are in close contact with their Adult and Nurturing permissions can help you here.

Remember, you are a born imitator. By choosing to imitate those who have the qualities you want to develop, you hasten the process of pro-life permissions becoming spontaneous reactions.

Be aware, however, that each time you go against the phantom Criticizer-in-your-head (especially at first) an "I'm doing something wrong; something naughty, forbidden" feeling may be triggered off inside you. This will happen even though your Adult rational mind knows it isn't naughty. Such a feeling can be tagged as coming straight from your earlier brainwashed Child, who is responding as if the present situation matches the past.

Injunctions against feelings

Far and away the most popular of the Critizer's injunctions is its edict against feelings. For some of you the command was against all feelings—positive or negative. You were taught to play the tune of life strictly on middle C.

You may have been programmed into expressing only positive feelings. The problem here is that feelings are tied together. To the extent that negatives are held in your positive emotions cannot flow freely.

An integral part of your person is your particular feeling at the moment. Each time you deny a wish, hurt, longing, fear, frustration, joy or any feeling you give up a vital and real part of the Experiencing You.

Biofeedback has shown that every feeling has a physical component. This means your body reacts to each feeling; your muscles and organs know the score. Unlike other things, buried feelings stay alive—very much alive. Unexpressed feelings get expressed in symptoms. An accumulation of denied feelings puts your body under tremendous stress. You avoid such stress when you ask yourself, "What message lies behind my symptom? What is my body trying to tell me?" And giving yourself permission to deal directly with it. Then you deal with your emotions, rather than having them deal with you. Such an approach puts you in the driver's seat.

Interesting research has shown that the cancer-prone personality is one who denies feelings. Such persons tend to carry masked anger beneath personalities described as "too good to be true," "never a complaint" or as "always giving to others at their own expense." Before the malignancy appears they often suffer a significant loss but deny their feelings about it.

Feelings simply are. They exist and need to be faced and dealt with constructively. The Nurturer gives permission for all feelings to exist.

As an adult you can now give yourself permission to lift past injunctions against feelings. You can choose to give yourself permission to let each emotion into your awareness without judgment. You also need to give yourself permission *not to act* on those that will have irresponsible consequences for you or others.

Emotional and physical well-being is directly tied to the degree to which you are in touch with all of your emotions. Just as you do not *act* on all of them, you do not necessarily share all of them with everyone. But you do not pretend they do not exist. You consciously create a real democracy in your awareness. You give each feeling freedom of speech in your head.

Feelings are like musical instruments. If you want to experience the full orchestra of life you don't take out the brasses and drums, featuring only the violins and woodwinds.

More hang-ups center around repressed feelings. We play the "If you really knew me" game. The "Unacceptable Me" is most often wrapped around the possession of some "naughty" feeling. Look carefully at your programming.

Were you still lovable in the eyes of those important others if you felt silly, shy, sad, tearful, hurt, pained, jealous, angry, scared, sexy, affectionate, tired, discouraged, overwhelmed, complaining, argumentative, feisty, rebellious, playful, happy, aggressive, assertive, excited, curious, frustrated, helpless, bossy, lonely, needing, discouraged, impatient? Which specific feelings were allowed you in childhood? Which brought disapproval? Which were modeled by your parents? Which did they avoid displaying?

Their way of handling their feelings, their way of handling your feelings play an important part in how you handle yours today. And whether you embrace your total "Feeling Me."

Here are some typical examples of how people become alienated from themselves.

It was natural for Norma to assert herself as a small child. But consistently she met sharp punishment each time she did. So she pushed down her assertiveness and felt something must be wrong with her for having such an unacceptable feeling.

Every holiday or vacation time brought on periods of strong tension for Dave. "Part of me feels excited and glad but another part feels tense. It's hard to sort the two out," he said. What he discovered was that his normal exuberance over special occasions in his childhood had been unacceptable to his father. How often he heard, "Getting in a dither over special days is for women and girls and sissies." To his father any normal joy or elation was regarded as "being in a dither" and quite unacceptable for a male.

Most men and many women are programmed early and hard that crying is a sign of weakness. We even laud the person who has lost a loved one through death as "being so brave" when they don't shed tears. "Keep a stiff upper lip" is an injunction many live with. "Be a good sport" often means "Pretend you don't feel disappointed when you lose." How often we hear someone say, "I broke down and cried!" as if that were a terrible admission.

Great numbers of people feel very unworthy, somehow less acceptable when they experience certain emotions. We often hear, "Oh, George is so emotionally stable; he never shows his emotions." What we may not know is that George is as alienated from his feeling Self as he is from others, that he suffers from asthma, ulcers, high blood pressure or migraines. But, man, is he cool!

We'll see in the next chapter how this leads to masking and role-playing which serves to cut us off from intimacy with others. At this point, just remember that the injunction "Don't feel" says "Invalidate a real part of yourself." It is the cause of the disowned Self.

Every normal person has had every unacceptable feeling from time to time. To deny this is to deny your humanness. Self-esteem comes with not having to disown any emotion, thought or desire. You assume ownership of them all and work to handle them constructively and responsibly. The only way we command Nature is to obey her, not deny her. Remember, repressed feelings control you. Expressed appropriately, you control them.

In Chapter Four the Child's fear of intimacy was mentioned. Too many of us learned very early that to reveal feelings to impor-

tant others was to have them denied or censured. Maybe it even
meant punishment or rejection. So we closed up. And thereby we
set our feet on the path of alienation—from ourselves, from others.

**To the extent you hide your feelings
you are alienated from yourself and others.
And your loneliness is proportional.**

A simple yet effective way to break through any negative conditioning you may have about your emotions is to get in touch with
each feeling of the moment, state it to yourself and add, "And
that's OK."

In a ten-minute period your feeling-barometer might register
frustration, jealousy, restlessness and then fascination. As each emotion surfaces into awareness, your inner dialogue would go,

At this moment I feel frustrated. *And that's OK.*
At this moment I feel jealous. *And that's OK.* (Jealousy
only masks feeling unlucky in some area.)
At this moment I feel restless. *And that's OK.*
At this moment I feel fascination. *And that's OK.*

What's the purpose of such seemingly strange talk? You are simply reparenting yourself with the Nurturer's Voice which was the
one that would originally have allowed you to "own" your total
"Feeling Me." To repeat, you can rewrite your own tapes regardless
of your past programming. The crucial phrase, "And that's OK,"
will become the new Voice canceling out the old judgmental one
that has brought pain and guilt and kept you fractionated.

Let's look now at how fears of revealing result in the decision to
mask and role-play.

TEN

ROLE OR REAL

Appear or be

The Critical Parent Voice is highly concerned with *appearances*. Its strong injunction is "Don't experience what you do experience." Unlike the Nurturer, it stresses the "good front." It rewards play-acting.

From our earliest days to varying degrees we are unintentionally taught not to heed our inner experience.

> "Eat" when you were full or not hungry.
> "Don't cry" when you suffered a loss.
> "Tell your sister you're sorry" when you weren't.
> "There's nothing to be afraid of" when you were scared stiff.
> "See it my way" when you honestly couldn't.
> "Sit still" when your muscles screamed for activity.
> "Enjoy it" when the activity or lesson bored you to tears.
> "Don't worry; it will be all right" when you were torn with concern.
> "It doesn't hurt" when the shot stung.
> A slap when you reached to explore.

The list of pretend's you were bombarded with is endless. And gradually you turned a deaf ear to your body's messages. Many of these edicts left you feeling guilty, bad or wrong because you couldn't inwardly buy them.

The great cocoon

Early in life then a covering-up process begins.

Who you *are* (the Experiencing You) becomes encased with who you *fear* you are (the "Unacceptable" You-that-didn't-fit-the-mold-they-wanted).

Your fear layer is then hidden behind who you *pretend* to be (the Masked, Role-playing You). You erect a Pretend Self to present to others. And your façade is tied to the expectations and injunctions of important others and the culture around you.

Role-playing helps you connect with others while guaranteeing that your fear layer is protected. To your Inner Child who needs the safety of acceptance

Appearing becomes more important than being.

The pretend layer is basically simply a survival strategy. Yet role-playing means keeping the parts of you that don't fit the required stereotype under wraps. Regardless of the acceptance the façade brings, you know that approval is for the unreal.

The tragedy is that as adults we believe the mask adopted earlier still helps us survive as it once did. The reality is that it is anti-life.

"Inside me there's a little voice that's so sure. It constantly reminds me that I'm incapable, not so bright and that I'll goof. (Critical Parent tape.)

"So I've spent most my life being super careful that others see me as happy, productive and outgoing. People tell me how much they admire me but I keep thinking, 'If they only knew.' Their compliments are for my act and God alone knows how highly polished it is. 'The big act' is the story of my life. But no one knows the strain it is. Or how utterly lonely I feel inside sometimes."

Do you live with a variation of Tom's tune?

If so, you weave a tight cocoon that can eventually cut you off from your own Inner Beingness.

Roles become real

Façades can become so real that some of us lose touch with our Real Selves. We deny to others and ourselves that the unreal is not us. The longer we play roles, the harder it is to let them go. When and if we finally release them, we may find we have little or no sense of Selfhood apart from them.

When you fuse your identity to the Pretend You—an adopted stance—you think you share yourself with others. But instead you only reel off the words and feelings that fit the mask you wear. You may not reveal even to yourself the lie you live. And so,

**You become role
rather than real.**

An enormous number of people have little or no sense of Selfhood apart from their roles.

Jenny went into a deep depression when her children were on their own. She had hidden completely behind her role first as a "good" daughter and then as a "good" mother. The empty nest left her without a reason for being.

Bob floundered miserably with retirement. His identity centered around wage-earning. Without his role as a worker in industry he was lost.

"I feel like a nonentity since my divorce," said Peggy. Her identity was built on being half of a couple.

Warren lived with the strong conviction that he was unlovable because of the unpretty feelings he harbored beneath his "nice guy" act.

To pull away from role fusion or avoid it, to reclaim your autonomy, give yourself the Nurturer's permission to see yourself *first and foremost as a person* and secondarily as being involved in certain personal or work relationships. Regardless of your work or relationships you are above all You—a fully human Being who may or may not experience what "they" tell you you *ought* to experience.

It is crucial to avoid
becoming one with any role.

Role stereotypes

It is easy to read about role fusion and nod acknowledgment. But go back to the list of self-expectations you made in Chapter Six. Re-examine the "should's" you hold for being a wife, husband, man, woman, parent, friend, in-law, secretary, teacher, dentist and so on.

Often these "should's" are based on role ideals or stereotypes. Check your list and ask, "How much role-playing am I involved in?" "How often do I hide what I really experience because it doesn't fit the mold of what I think I am 'supposed' to feel in this situation?"

Our culture is steeped in role stereotypes. Men must hide their feelings of weakness, fear, disappointment, tenderness and hurt. Or their masculinity is questioned. Be tough, compete aggressively, win, drive for material success; that's the American ideal. The man who buys this image wouldn't be caught dead changing a diaper, washing a dish or shedding a tear. Intimate communication is out. It takes a strong male in our culture to run counter to these stereotypes. Some men, especially in our younger generation, are beginning to push out of this mold.

Strength and assertiveness in women have long been no-no's that present-day groups are challenging. Why is a woman's femininity tied to whether she wields a broom or a shovel? Hopefully women's liberation will lead to men's liberation and our major concern will be person liberation.

Basically roles subjugate human Be-ingness to a tight package of expectations. And should you feel constrained or restless in that box, you may well be told that something is the matter with you. That's been the official cultural attitude. Only recently have we been questioning stereotypes of all kinds rather than the persons wanting to wriggle free of them. The emergence of human Be-ingness is fortunately beginning to be sanctioned but not without much static.

Giving up role-playing doesn't mean you give up handling your relationships responsibly.

A teacher has an assigned task to help students learn. And she shirks if she fails to follow through. But if she sees herself as a *person who happens to be teaching,* she doesn't adopt the standard mannerisms and stance of the stereotype. She can afford to

> apologize if she makes a mistake (she doesn't play perfect) ;
> admit she doesn't know (she doesn't play encyclopedia) ;
> show all human feelings (she doesn't play robot) ;
> tolerate different opinions (she doesn't play God) ;
> change her mind (she doesn't play rigid) ;
> care (she doesn't play distant) ;
> ask for help (she doesn't play invincible).

Revealing and love

Shedding the pretend layer is scary. It means revealing who you're afraid you are. But remember, *that fear layer was created from early childhood impressions in a context that no longer exists.*

Until you risk revealing your fear layer, you can never test the childhood myth of the "Unacceptable Me." *The great fallacy is your belief that others will reject your inner stuff just as you have.*

The experience of sharing your "Unacceptable Me" in a self-chosen safe climate is worth the risk. It's the only way to dispel the fantasy once and for all. Amazingly, instead of the old rejections, you're most likely to find acceptance, psychological intimacy and love. Setting aside the fear layer allows the beauty that is truly You (and it has been there all along) to shine out.

A word of caution, however. Remember, if you inwardly reject your own feelings, dreams and wants, you (your Not-OK Child) are unconsciously most likely to choose to reveal yourself to someone who will join hands with your Inner Criticizer. You'll choose to open up to someone who plays Judgmental Parent.

Katie, for example, unconsciously chose to share her real feelings with a critical friend rather than with her more empathic one.

"Maggie," she said, "I sometimes feel as if my kids are driving me up the wall!"

"How can you say that about those two sweet children?" asked Maggie.

"Sweet! They bicker and tease from morning till night. And as fast as I get the place cleaned up they leave a trail a mile wide. And they never seem to take no for an answer. They make such a fuss I finally give in. Half the time I feel like bursting into tears!"

Maggie frowned firmly. "Katie, you'd better get hold of yourself! Thousands of mothers have lived through the pre-school years and don't go to pieces over such simple things. Just think of all the poor women who'd like to have children and can't have them."

"Well, some days I'd willingly give them mine," burst Katie.

"My word, Katie, that is a dreadful thing to say. If anything ever happened to them you'd never forgive yourself for having such horrible thoughts!"

"You're right," said Katie, tears sliding down her face. "I'm an awful mother and I should be ashamed of myself. It's my fault that I'm so impatient. They don't mean to be trouble; after all, they are just children. I feel so terribly guilty for having said these things."

Maggie's every response to Katie's feelings was straight from her Critical Parent tape. She blamed, judged and condemned so that Katie's "Unacceptable Me" got the very reinforcement it needed to continue playing Pretend. That night when Katie went to bed she could scarcely sleep she was so overwhelmed with guilt. And she firmly resolved not to share such feelings again. She'd play Always Loving Mother.

Had Katie not had a need to be put down, she wouldn't have chosen to open up to Maggie, who she knew was an extremely critical person. If instead she had shared with Julie, whom she experienced as much more understanding, she wouldn't have collected the guilt feelings she unconsciously needed. Instead the dialogue might have gone this way:

"Julie, I sometimes feel as if my kids are driving me up the wall!"

"You've just had it with those two, Katie," said Julie.

"You can say that again. They bicker and tease from morning till night. And as fast as I get the place cleaned up they leave a trail a mile wide. And they never seem to take no for an answer. They make such a fuss I finally give in. Half the time I feel like bursting into tears!"

"Gee, honey, you feel defeated and overwhelmed," empathized Julie.

"That's for sure. I guess it's partly that Jim has been working overtime a lot so I haven't seen much of him or had his help. And when he does come home lots of times he's so shot that he's cross with me and I just feel I can't take any more pressure."

"Not having his support is bad enough. But having him be cross feels like the last straw," said Julie.

"Yeah," said Katie more calmly. "Honestly, I hate to say this, but sometimes I don't think I was cut out to be a mother."

"You know, Katie, I can remember so clearly having the same feelings when my kids were at the stage yours are. I felt so inadequate to cope."

"You did?" Katie's eyes went wide. "Gosh, I thought something was the matter with me. Maybe what Jim and I need is a weekend away together with no responsibilities and just having fun together."

Sharing with a non-judgmental friend would allow Katie the relief of unloading feelings without collecting guilt. It would have helped her to a constructive solution to her fatigue and frustration —something she needed badly.

Not everyone can tolerate openness and to expect such is to set yourself up for disappointment. It can reinforce your need to mask. Selecting empathic listeners allows you to drop your mask, reveal those "Awful" feelings and find the warmth from an understanding heart.

Keeping your "Awful Self" tucked away in a secret compartment also means others are less likely to share with you. The unreal does not breed the real. Appropriate sharing helps others feel safe to disclose themselves to you. And real closeness is what we all need.

Masks and genuine intimacy are incompatible.

You already know that love given for your façade is not nurturing because the mask is not You. The love you receive when you share your fear layer is for real.

Masking requires enormous energy and guardedness. Spontaneity and free development of your potential go by the boards. Living out role expectations is a commitment that wipes out Self nurturing.

Question yourself searchingly. How often are you pretending to be (the Critical injunction)? How often are you being appropriately real (the Nurturing permission)?

Challenging myths

Many of the self-limiting ideas you live with may not have been modeled or taught. They are blueprints you concocted from early childish impressions. And you failed to challenge them as you grew older.

A son or daughter can never rise beyond the father or mother.

Two people in the same home cannot be competent.

It is disloyal to be strong if the parent you like is weak.

To enjoy something the parent you reject enjoys means you become like that parent in all respects.

It is bad to reject something the preferred parent enjoyed.

The list of such myths is long and necessarily personal to you. Since such myths dampen what you permit for yourself, it is important to ferret them out. What are some of the myths you allow to stymie your fully experiencing and expressing your Self?

Such myths often center around separateness and comparisons as we seek to establish our identity. They are frequently variations of these themes:

It is not all right to have a separate identity, *or*

The only way to have a separate identity is to be opposite from some significant other, *or*

It is not all right to be like "them" in some ways and unlike "them" in others.

Know that you are separate and unique. Know that you can never be like anyone else nor can others be like you. Know that you do not add to or take away from another by being true to your separate uniqueness. This knowledge gives you permission to be your own person.

The most important knowing is that

**You do not need someone else
to give you pro-life permissions.**

As an adult you can give them to yourself.

Survival roles

Let's look at some roles that are commonly played. Some of these have been considered earlier in terms of self-expectancies. Now let's see them from the angle of ways we handle the basic fear-layer belief, "I am unlovable." To your Inner Child unlovability is tantamount to death. To prevent that psychological death (the Inner Child believes it is literal death) it concocts a role or stance it believes is necessary for survival.

Virginia Satir* has suggested four such brave responses for survival:

PLACATER: Believing you are unlovable, you put your survival in others. You play "peace at any price"; therefore you buy blame and criticism to keep others quiet. You blur or blot out your needs. Your stance is, "You count; I don't." You play Victim and Submittee . . . anything to get those needed strokes.

BLAMER: Like the Placater you believe in your unlovability. Your survival is in others too. But it is dependent on your staying in power, on others being puppets. Others are used to shore up your desperate need to count. So you must blur or blot out others' needs if you are to stay on top. You act as if "I count; you don't," but this position is a defense against seeing your own fear layer of Not-OKness.

* Virginia Satir, *Peoplemaking*. Palo Alto, Ca.: Science & Behavior Books, 1972. (See pp. 63–72 for further detail on these roles.)

COMPUTER: To get into feelings is too frightening. Nailing down your own emotions, your survival depends on rules and things. So you are super objective; you remain wedded strictly to the Adult tape. You blur or blot out your own and others' human feelings. Only the rational counts. You don't deal with anything but head tripping.

DISTRACTER: Frightened of feelings, confrontation and reality your survival depends on blurring or blotting out the real issues—potatoes too hot to handle. You feel fragmented and avoidance is all that counts.

As Satir suggests, clinging tightly to any one survival stance prevents your being a free-flowing whole human being. Yet each position when used *appropriately* can be part of being authentic. When you are free you try to meet others' needs (but not at the consistent expense of your own). You choose to confront and disagree (but not with put-downs of the other). You are reasonable and objective at appropriate times (but not at the cost of denying feelings). Distractions appropriately used relieve tension.

Another way of putting this is that when we are whole, as we've seen, we are committed to Nurturing, Adult and Natural Child responses that fit the situation. We are not frozen into a particular stance—born of survival needs—that becomes our sole response in every situation.

Other survival roles† based on the unlovability fear layer are:

RESCUER: I'll convince myself and others I count by saving helpless souls who obviously couldn't make it without me.

ACHIEVER: My survival depends on collecting undeniable evidence of my worth through what I do.

OVERINDULGER: I can't stand your disapproval so I'll

† John Powell, *Why Am I Afraid to Tell You Who I Am?* Niles, Ill.: Argus, 1969. (See pp. 121–67 for an expanded discussion of these roles as well as additional ones.)

give endlessly. Bountiful giving also helps me avoid looking at my hidden rejections and resentments.

VANITY: My survival depends on the handsomeness or beauty of my outer package; that's is all I have to offer.

CLOWN: I can't afford to be serious or I'd have to face my own inner pain.

SUPERIOR: To avoid facing my unlovability I delude myself that I count more than you. Grandiose fantasies and always being right keep me from my real feelings of inferiority.

ESCAPER: It's hopeless to get what I need out there, but with daydreams, TV, books, food or chemicals I can ease the pain of my "Awful Me."

COOL CAT: A continual stream of admirers and one-night stands are the best way to run from inner pain and get lots of strokes without giving in return. I don't have anything to offer others.

DELICATE: If I play Handle-With-Care others won't ask much of me. I'm so inadequate I couldn't cope anyway. Even if I could, I don't want to try.

MARTYR: I collect "count" strokes by playing on others' guilt and pity. They have to appreciate all my sacrifices.

INDIFFERENT: Survival depends on not letting anyone know how much I hurt, care or want. I'll wall up.

There are dozens of other roles we may adopt. Each, however, springs off the basic need to deal with our lack of wholehearted self-acceptance. Each spawns from the need somehow to survive the Big Lie—"I am unlovable."

We probably all adopt some of these roles at times temporarily and, hopefully, are aware of when we do. But when we use them exclusively, we choose to hide and manipulate. Such a choice is only proof we've bought into a false Self Belief System.

Are you using others or yourself to patch up your survival raft? Remember,

Love
is not using.

When you affirm yourself, you do not use yourself or your relationships in ways that belittle or diminish your intrinsic worth—or that of others.

Sorting out

Part of growing up emotionally is sifting the wheat from the chaff. The sorting-out process is not easy nor done overnight. You can see it as a heavy trip or an exciting self-discovery process.

Start by asking yourself,

Does what I say or do spring from how I think a person ought to talk or act?

Or does it come from my genuine inner experience?

Am I using a brave response for survival role?

Am I investing in hiding my unlovability fears?

What's the worst that could happen if I open up and appropriately reveal the Experiencing Me?

Will I really drop dead if someone does reject me?

Does love for my "good front" really nurture me?

Fear of hurt

Practicing new responses means risking. The once-burned Child-in-you fears giving up its protective mask.

"I don't want to be hurt," it declares loudly.

A strange phenomenon is at work in us.

We bear many physical hurts: falls, shots, broken bones, illnesses, surgeries. But much as we dislike them, we do not closet ourselves to cower from such hurts in the future. We simply do not *expect* to go through life without physical hurts from time to time.

But let the hurts be psychological (disapproval or rejection) and we (the Child-in-us) recoil like frightened animals. Our approval-needing Child rules the stage. And we seal our inner selves away in isolation.

Vulnerability and self-rejection

We all know we can't go through life without disapproval or rejection periodically. But the time when rejection's sting becomes unbearable is when it joins our own self-rejection.

If each rejection cuts you to the bone, you need to look at why you are rejecting yourself. Invariably you'll find you've based your case on the negative self-image formed during your early years. Even if you were totally rejected by both parents, they are not the only people in the world.

Clinging to the Child's pain, the desperate fear of rejection, is a way to avoid the reality that you are no longer a child.

Surely closeness means hurt from time to time. But the hurt is less deep, less lasting when you basically affirm yourself. Becoming a Self Nurturer simply lessens the extent of your vulnerability to others.

The hurt is diminished when you realize that others, to some degree, always see you through their own needs. What they cannot accept in themselves they cannot accept in you. Their rejection of any part in you most often speaks of their rejection of that same part in themselves.

Yes, withdrawal and masks wall off vulnerability. But the cost is increasing isolation. The choice is clear. Vulnerability or masks. Hurts once in a while or loneliness all the time. Being or non-Being. Life or death.

Do you expect that living includes some psychological as well as physical hurts? That's reality. It's the Burned Child that believes it will perish if it reveals vulnerability.

Start by taking little steps. Reveal your true reactions in safe places at first. Soon you may find yourself willing to take larger risks in less safe places. You create the largest "safe place" for yourself when you tie your self-talk to the Nurturer, Adult and Natural Child within.

Handling vulnerability

We've already talked about the process for dealing with feelings constructively. The pain that comes when a sensitive spot is hit needs to be faced. You simply give yourself the Nurturer's permission to "sit in the feeling."

Keep in mind that

Healing only comes
with discharge in a safe place.

Turning to an empathic person to work out hurts is almost always more helpful than working them through alone. But this is not always necessary.

"I've always been terrified of being alone," said Rose. "So I usually keep myself busy and around others from morning till night even though that's been exhausting. One night I decided to face the loneliness. I knew if the pain got too much I could call a friend. I just sat there and let the fear come. It came in waves. Old painful memories of loneliness in childhood came flooding back. But I stayed with them. In one way it felt good to stop running and just let the tears and hurt come. I was amazed that the very worst was over in about twenty minutes. By bedtime I knew I'd never be afraid of being alone again. It seemed such a waste when I thought of the years I'd spent running from it. And I was amazed. My *fear* of the pain was far greater than experiencing it."

As is almost inevitably the case, the Inner Child's fear is greater than the adult experience of that very same fear. But you don't discover this fact until you face the hurt. To erase it you need to face it.

Welcoming your opposites

Part of returning to realness is giving yourself permission to welcome your opposites. How often we hear such statements as

Jim is a patient guy.

Marilyn's so thoughtful.

Grace is really aggressive.

Yet if you follow Jim hourly, you find that at times he behaves impatiently. Marilyn's every act is not thoughtful. Nor does Grace behave aggressively in all situations.

We've all had the label trip laid on us from our earliest days. And we consequently make "either-or" statements about ourselves. Your Critical Parent tends to see you with "either-or" eyes. To it you are either good *or* bad, kind *or* unkind, selfish *or* unselfish. You are branded as one way *or* the other.

The Criticizer categorizes. It does not see that you behave differently depending on the situation and the emotional load you carry at the moment.

You increase Self nurturing when you see yourself more accurately. You behave in various ways: kind *and* unkind, giving *and* withholding, outgoing *and* shy, *depending on the situation.* You don't pigeonhole yourself with either-or categories unless you see yourself with the Criticizer's eye. Surely, you may display one quality more frequently. But do not deny the total reality of your behavior by squeezing your self-picture into rigid categories.

Anyone who always displays only one side of a particular trait or emotion has simply repressed its opposite. And such repression does not allow you to be real.

You and I cannot be fully self-confident winners until our self-view includes our polarities—our opposites. The Nurturing Voice gives us that permission; it does not slap us into either-or boxes. It knows that as human beings we are capable of all degrees and fluctuations of every human emotion and trait.

Positive action

As you lift off the constrictors ("should's," unreal expectations, self-judgments, injunctions, roles and survival tactics), it is equally important to take active steps to be a loving friend to You.

Be aware that your Criticizer and Not-OK Child will challenge each friendly gesture as being undeserved or deserved "only if . . ."

By knowing where that Voice comes from you can choose to hear it out but not pay it homage. You can say, "Yes, dear. I hear what you're saying, but I choose to set you aside."

Let's look at constructive ways to befriend yourself.

· ELEVEN ·

A FRIEND FOR YOU

Friendship

Think of someone you regard as a dear friend. If no such person exists for you, dream one up.

You know that time spent with such a friend brings (or would bring) a special kind of joy. You tend to be solicitous, protective and loving toward him or her. You have the other's best interests at heart. You care.

Now mentally review the specific favors you extend to express your caring to this dear one. Then ask yourself, "Do I give myself the same tender consideration?"

On the basis of our own self-treatment, many of us would truthfully need to answer, "Certainly not!" If this is your answer, ask yourself why.

As we've seen, if your Critical Parent and Not-OK Child are strong you've had a vested interest in being anything but friendly toward you. This inner masochism has caused you unconsciously to engineer defeats and deprivations that consciously leave you feeling victimized.

If you've been practicing the ideas here, you've given up co-operating with past negative programming. Now let's look at some additional ways to be your own best friend.

Friendliness toward your body

Your Critical Parent with its incessant demands and expectations indirectly sanctions your being very hard on your physical body. If you avoid your Adult Voice, you deny reality by believing you can disregard health rules and still feel vital and strong. Part of Self nurturing means taking good care of yourself physically.

Most of us are tremendously disrespectful of our bodies' needs. We may put only the finest grade of oil and gasoline in our cars. But we completely deny our physical machinery equal care. We load our bodies with devitalized food (cheap gas), drive them relentlessly, refuse them adequate rest and tension-releasing exercise. We bulldoze them through one stress situation after another at high speed.

For a quick check on how your body feels about your treatment up to now, have a dialogue with it. Either a mental conversation or preferably a written one. Let your body speak first. Write, "I am your body and I feel . . ." You may be surprised to learn how angry it is with you, how "unfaired against" it feels. Then talk back to your body and check out how you respond to its requests. Let the dialogue flow. When it is finished, ask your body what it really wants from you. Ask yourself if it is really fair to expect to "get" from your body if you regularly fail to "give" to it.

This is part of what emerged from Nell's dialogue with her body.

BODY: I am your body and I feel tied up in knots.

NELL: What on earth for? I take good care of you, so you have no reason to feel that way.

BODY: Don't tell me what I'm going through. And I don't have to have a reason. All I know is that my muscles are tighter than a drum. It feels as if I want to scream, but you keep smiling and pushing down this screaming part.

NELL: I don't even know what you're talking about.

BODY: That's the problem. You refuse to let me talk or

to listen to me. The other day when that woman made that snide remark at you, it hurt inside me. But you just smiled and acted like my hurt wasn't there. But I feel it. And what am I supposed to do with all these feelings?

NELL: I can't understand what you are talking about.

BODY: Of course you can't. You keep acting as if what's happening inside me isn't happening. But I'm reaching the bursting point and I'm afraid I'll get sick before long.

Characteristically, Nell denied her feelings. Consciously she didn't experience many of them. But the fact that another part of her did register them came out as she wrote in far greater detail.

Here's a portion of Art's dialogue:

BODY: I am your body and I feel worn out. Why won't you give me a break once in a while:

ART: Oh, knock it off. You're supposed to work for me. You get all you need from me, so quit whimpering.

BODY: Art, I'm very tired of the rat race you drive me through every day. You seem to think you can shove me through loops without rest. You'd never treat your beloved motorcycle that way. Man, you take the best care of it possible. How come I don't get some of the same consideration?

ART: I can't stop. My job demands that I go full speed. And when I get home my wife and kids always put a thousand demands on me. And there's that infernal yard work that never lets up.

BODY: Tell me another one. What's going to happen to your job and your wife and kids and your dichondra when I drop under the pressure you're pouring on?

Why not check out your body dialogue to see what you come up with?

Giving to your body, of course, means following all the general rules for keeping fit—a nutritious diet, adequate sleep and exercise and physical checkups. It also means not demanding more than your particular body can physically deliver. You refuse to run your engine at high speed month after month. If your work involves a lot of pressure, you actively plan buffer periods—specific breaks that allow you to disengage completely and recoup. And that doesn't mean once a year. Spots during your day are slotted for "unwind" and you let only dire emergencies interfere. We all need saunter time at points during the day.

Only you know what you can comfortably handle. If a job's pressures are more than you can handle, you seriously question taking it on. You permit yourself to say "No," to avoid overextending.

This gentleness is easier when you refuse perfectionism and actively set up priorities in the order of their importance. It is easier when you give up seeking OKness by culturally defined externals. Seriously look at what you may be avoiding or running from by keeping yourself consistently under the gun.

Reclaim your Adult

We each have an Adult within. We either use it or we don't. We either check with reality or we don't. We either make choices that are for or against us and others. We either think ahead to logical consequences or we do not.

When the long-range goal means giving up a present pleasure, our Adult helps us with self-discipline. We learn then to say "No" firmly to the Impulsive Child within.

Inevitably each of us needs to develop moral standards—ethical codes—to live by. When our behavior falls below that standard either we correct the behavior or we pay the price.

Part of being your own friend means reclaiming your Adult so that it becomes an active yet flexible Voice in your inner dialogue. This Voice helps you behave responsibly to yourself and others.

Your Natural Child

Your Natural Child enjoys and needs free, spontaneous play.

How much play time do you allow yourself? How long has it been since you gave yourself permission to frolic?

Too many of us put aside childish pleasure with adulthood. Play for us means trying to win at games or watching others do the same. Whether it's bowling or tennis, golf or bridge, softball or dancing, the pressure is on how you perform.

"Yes, but I enjoy sports competition and it works off my tensions," you say.

No argument. Physical activity that you enjoy is all to the good. And it's fun to do well in any recreational outlet. But when you participate with "should's" on your back or remain a spectator, that is not play as defined and needed by your Natural Child.

Think back to your very early years. Play meant you could be silly, imaginative, impulsive, creative and drop an activity when it stopped being fun. You flowed freely with the intrinsic joy of the activity without plan or purpose. You focused on delight, not achievement or scores.

All too early we are programmed to compete in play. That has its advantages and disadvantages. But we need to make a clear separation between achievement-play and Natural Child play.

Watch a five-year-old run at the beach. Like a playful puppy she revels in the very sensations of joyous activity. Watch an adult run on the beach. There's little glee. She's grimly determined to build up a muscle, increase her stamina or pound off fat.

High self-esteemers keep their Natural Child very much alive. Their spontaneous childlike delight is very evident. Joy in the sheer doing marks their play.

To reconnect with your Natural Child, think back to what gave you delight as a small child. Foolish for grownups? Who says? Invariably it will be the Critical Voice. Duck under it; hang loose and let your Natural Child enjoy the exhilaration of pure fun.

Another characteristic of your Natural Child is its openness to all the senses. Think back. Do you remember the experience of:

Running through a meadow with the wind in your hair?
Tearing across a field while your kite zigged and zagged?
Giggling with joy as you mouthed a new word?
Feeling the swish as you raced down a slide?
Sharing tall tales by the light of a fire?

Tuning in to the pillow as you drifted to sleep?
Playing with bubbles in a long soaky bath?
Watching the shadows dance on the leaves?
Sniffing the orange as you peeled off the skin?
Hearing the noise of the puddling of rain?
Absorbing the quiet of snowfall at night?
Running your finger—kerthump—on the fence?
Feeling the water caress as you swam?
Rolling a caramel around in your mouth?
Making up cloud stories in the wind-molded shapes?
Snuggling up close to the warmth of your dog?

Delight in fully experiencing each day means staying in close touch with all of your senses. What a great loss when you fail to enjoy them. Your ability to recapture is there for the taking. You need only give your Natural Child permission to come out from under its wraps.

"Only that day dawns to which we are awake," said Thoreau. And many of us keep whole decades of our lives soundly asleep. Each day comes and goes; yet the beauty of its momentary dawnings is lost when we walk unawake.

Recall what gave you pleasure as a child. Or seemed as if it would have been fun if you had been allowed to do it. Make an agreement with yourself to do a few of those things each week. Schedule at least one per week.

Your Natural Child is enormously curious and creative. Negative programming often totally squelches these aspects of your Being. But that curiosity and creativity are still inside. Self nurturing includes welcoming back these parts of yourself.

To do this, give yourself specific permission to get involved with body movement or dance, with music (both the listening and producing), with art in all its many forms, with writing or playing with words. Allow yourself to investigate hobbies or activities you think you might enjoy or did enjoy as a child.

Mary's younger sister was outstanding at sports. Physically less endowed, Mary concluded that since she was not good at the games she would not get involved. At fifty she decided to take up tennis. She had always thought it looked like fun. She found a soul sister and they played by Mary's rules: no serving, no attention paid to the lines on the court, hits allowed on any bounce. And the only score kept was how many times the ball went over the net. These two women opened up a whole new avenue of fun for themselves.

"But don't you feel embarrassed when others are waiting for the court?" asked a friend.

"No," replied Mary. "I just remind myself how good I make the onlookers feel if they need to compare me with them. I use my twenty minutes on the court to enjoy the feel of my muscles moving."

Mary's attitude underscores the only requirement for encouraging your Natural Child. Remember, you completely set aside the idea of producing or achieving up to some external standard. Your focus is on the joy of experiencing. If someone asks you what you are making as you swish with finger paints or play with clay, tell them, "I'm making fun."

Permitting yourself to play freely and spontaneously may be hard at first. If so, in the beginning it may be easier to let your Natural Child out during alone time. Or by getting involved in classes where the teacher supports experiencing rather than producing or achieving.

If learning new things intrigues you, you avoid the perform-or-get-out trap by taking non-credit classes. It's easier to risk venturing into the new if success or failure is not a consideration. Remember, you are simply there for the experience, to discover what speaks to you. The Nurturing Voice supports curiosity, fun and creativity. You can give this gift to yourself.

Gifts to you

What do you consistently give yourself that could qualify as a gift?

Some periodic indulgences that are friendly gestures to yourself involve a little extra spending. If that can be worked into your budget, let yourself buy that new record, treat yourself to dinner out, hire someone to wash your windows.

This does not mean playing Indulged Child—squandering so that only self-interest is served. We're talking about gifts you give yourself that do not irresponsibly deprive others. *If self-indulgence has been your life theme, this section is not for you.*

Many of the gifts you can give yourself don't cost a cent. A little nap, allowing yourself to linger over a cup of coffee, a quiet stroll, a candlelight dinner, a special dish you particularly enjoy, window-shopping, time to finish the newspaper, fixing a garden bouquet for your own enjoyment . . . such gifts are ways of being friendly to You.

Most of us extend little kindnesses to others. The point is do you extend the same to yourself once in a while? Just because you want to be friendly to You? In short, how loving are you to You? Ask yourself, "How friendly have I been to me today?"

Make a specific list of the friendly gestures you presently extend to yourself. Compare it with your earlier list of kindnesses to others. Are they noticeably out of balance? If so, why?

If you give only to others, you may put your need to receive as a claim on them. Part of being a Self Nurturer means you don't cut yourself off your own friendship list. High self-esteemers give to others within limits. And they also periodically give to themselves.

Newly gained self-respect is often fragilely held. Carefully protect it, especially at first. Avoid situations and people who knock it down. If arrows come your way, imagine them glancing off or bypassing. You hold the power to absorb them or not.

Consciously question hero worship. It is a subtle self-put-down. Admiring and respecting certain qualities is different from seeing the other as superior to you.

Ask yourself, "How do I keep myself from experiencing pleasure?" Often we've been brainwashed with guilt about feeling good. If this fits for you tell yourself you deserve to feel happy just because you are a human being.

Remember, being kind to You means pleasing the whole You, the Nurturer, the Adult, the Natural Child. This means *irresponsible* self-pleasuring is out.

Present, past or future

Your Natural Child's focus is very much in the present rather than on the past or future. Its present-orientation needs to be coupled, of course, with Adult awareness if you are to function fully.

You make pain for yourself if you focus only on the dead past or the imagined direness of the future. Part of being your own friend involves learning from the past and planning realistically for the future. But you do not live exclusively in either or both time zones. You do not mar the present by wallowing in "if only" or "what if." Why?

Your Criticizer keeps you nailed to the past by beating you with the wisdom of hindsight. It constantly rehashes the hash; it refuses to release. Since it has little faith in you or others it keeps you on edge with fantasies about what can go wrong on the path ahead.

No one can change the past. "But," you say, "I can't forget it." You can choose to release it if you refuse to let your Critical Parent send you daily memos about it.

Imagining the worst ahead only makes it more likely to happen and is strictly a Critical Parent pastime.

It sometimes helps when you hear yourself on the "if only" or "what if" wave length to give this Voice space but on your terms. Make an appointment with yourself for a selected period (each day if necessary) to sit down and focus exclusively on the past or future or both. Tape-record or write out your thoughts.

What you will probably find is that these dialogues are monotonously similar. Over and over and over we replay certain scenes and we never move from there. Objective evidence of your broken record may help you release it. If not, exaggerate your dialogue. If it still remains, ask yourself what your payoff is for the constant repetition. You'll surely find one.

Your payoff is likely to be that each replay gives you a renewed dose of remorse, shame, guilt, worry or other Not-OK feelings. Estimate the number of hours you've clocked to date with the obsession of these themes. Remind yourself that not even the world's greatest tragedies are worth that many repeats. These grindings are like sitting in a rocking chair. They give you something to do but you get nowhere. They lock you into pain.

You tap into your Adult when you decide you cannot redo the past nor fully control the future. But for as long as your negative Voices want to hold forth, consciously give them time to speak. When their appointment time is over, you take charge. If they overstay or try to work in extra time, tell them you'll listen only during their next appointment period. You can consciously control where you put your focus. The present is the only time you really have.

Check your reaction to reading this book. As you've become more aware, as you have started choosing to be "for" rather than "against" yourself, as you have started feeling better, did you feel a sense of waste? As you looked back at your handling of educational opportunities, friendships, marriage, parenting, work, were you saddened? Have you stayed wedded to the thought, "If only I'd known this earlier?"

If so, remind yourself that earlier your awareness was limited. You did your best within that limitation. Remember the prisoner we spoke of in the second chapter who could have walked free had he known his cell door was unlocked? Once he had that awareness and walked clear he could have chosen to weep the rest of his life over his lost years. Or he could rejoice that his future was free.

Growth is a process. And life is what's happening while you are making the trip. Take time to stand on the edge of your psychological cocoon and share your feelings with it in silent, written or spoken dialogue. Know too that freedom tastes sweeter to those who have known the pain of confinement. "If only" keeps you from savoring today's joy.

Befriending your Child

Sometimes your Child may feel overwhelmed by negatives and take control of your stage.

You befriend your Child by asking it to focus on what advantages the negative event has. Invariably in every disadvantage there is an advantage. And you help the Child key into it.

Believing you can

An important characteristic of the Nurturing Voice is its positive faith in you. It believes you "can." Part of being your own friend is choosing the Nurturer's stance toward yourself. And you make that faith concrete by taking time for positive picturing.

This means getting in a comfortable position, closing your eyes and vividly *seeing* yourself (as if on a movie screen) doing or being or possessing the qualities you desire. In imagination you run this "can do" movie over and over (for at least ten to fifteen minutes) daily.

As you do this, identify with that picture. Become one with it. Say to yourself, "I am ———," using the trait or quality you are claiming. End the visualization with the attitude-expectation that this quality is now yours. The blueprint is

**See it;
become one with it;
claim it as yours.**

Top sports pros and countless others have found positively visualizing themselves making that perfect shot even more effective than actual practice sessions! You feel inadequate? Hear those feelings out. Then consciously set them aside and visualize yourself as confident and functioning appropriately in specific situations. You'll likely be surprised at the genuine positive shift in how you behave. Why?

When your Criticizer or Inadequate Voices are on, they continually whisper or shout "can't do's" to you. And you act accordingly. Visualizing the "can's" stills their voices. And you will tend to live up to your new positive images, just as the child tends to live up to his parents' or teachers' faith.

Actually seeing yourself in possession of the qualities you want carries more weight than making positive statements to yourself, as was mentioned in Chapter Seven. They give you positive subconscious experience rather than simply a verbal head trip. Within the bounds of the natural laws of the universe,

What you believe you can do, you will be likely to do.

Dr. Carl Simington's work with cancer patients dramatically underscores the power of positive picturing. His patients spend fifteen minutes twice daily vividly picturing their white blood cells attacking the tumor cells. The results have been extremely exciting. Cancer patients who believe that radiation will help are more likely to respond than those convinced it is useless.

No doubt you are familiar with the "placebo effect." Many patients get better when their doctors tell them a mere sugar pill is a powerful medicine that will definitely cure them. While those given a curative medication with the statement, "I doubt this will help but let's try it," often show no improvement. The sheer will to live has made the difference between life and death for many.

Never underestimate the power of your mind. Your thoughts and beliefs not only affect your hormonal system, they can be used to mobilize your positive potentials for living. Affirmative belief coupled with the necessary action puts you on the winner's path.

Focus out; go slowly

A tendency of many low- and mid-self-esteemers is to take themselves too seriously. There is a possibility if you tend to be intense that in reading this book, you will suddenly flip from non-awareness to total and complete introspection. You will hold the magnifying glass on every thought, feeling, act and relationship.

The word from here is take it easy. Take a step at a time, a day at a time. Developing a positive self-image is a gradual process. Don't pressure yourself to "arrive" all at once. You'll never make it. Great craftsmen work steadily on their creations but they don't get frantic over completion. Give yourself space and time to rework your self-picture.

Meantime, relax, enjoy and focus out. Get involved in activities you enjoy and have fun. That's part of being a friend to You.

If you are tempted to measure the movement you've made, use a broad time range. See yourself today as compared to five, ten or fifteen years ago. Remember the story of the hare and the tortoise. Slow and steady won the race. As long as you work consistently, you'll get there. Remember, Rome wasn't built in a day.

Go after what you want

For years you may have gone after what your parents, teachers or culture told you to want. That may or may not have matched what you want for You. Consciously step into your Nurturer and tenderly ask the Child within, "Honey, what would you like?"

Your Child, of course, may come up with items your Adult knows are out of the question. If so, hear the request but gently set it aside. It's friendship, not overindulgence, we're considering.

Part of self-friendship will be not heeding the Inadequate Child, who is used to going after the impossible in order to fail. Check out Child goals to see that they are not tied to the Criticizer's impossible ideals.

If you are a bit chubby and think you want to lose weight, ask yourself why. Is Twiggy your ideal or do you feel more comfortable and energetic when you are slimmer?

Peggy had big bones and solid muscles. Weighing 120 might be her ideal but it left her exhausted and weak. At 140 she wore a larger dress size but she felt better. She needed to question the cultural ideal against her own physical experience.

The new energy available from dropping the Criticizer and Inadequate tapes can now be directed outward. High self-esteemers enjoy scaling realistic challenges. Not to prove their value. But for the sheer fun of working them through. Small or large, you gift yourself when you choose challenges that intrigue you—not others —and pick up the glove.

In going after what you want, head for small, specific goals, little steps that gradually move you ahead. Instead of going off all fattening food forever, give up breadstuff for five days out of seven. Avoid insisting your whole house be clean. (Whose house but the perfectionist's is totally clean all the time?) Do one room or one closet and give yourself a mental trophy.

If you have family obligations and want more education, take a course or two at a time. What difference does it make that others get a degree in four years and it takes you eight? An old saying puts it clearly, "The journey of a thousand miles starts with the first step." Give yourself permission to take one step at a time. Play slow and easy. Play gentle with your self-expectancies as you move to meet your wants.

Alone or lonely

The word "alone" is a contraction of all and one. Once you throw out your destructive programming you welcome your all-oneness, your aloneness.

Loneliness comes when you continually go back to the same old rejecting source to not get what you've always not gotten.* Loneliness means sinking into the teachings of the Critical Parent and the feelings of the Not-OK Child. What you've always not gotten from those tapes is the good feelings of affirmation and validation for yourself. It means you are less likely to be able to give those gifts to others. Harry feels lonely most of the time. Yet his loud Critical Parent tape guarantees he'll stay there. His impossible expectations of others, his focus on others' flaws, his discomfort when his "due me's" don't materialize, his need to blame and dominate, his refusal to reveal his vulnerabilities or get involved all serve to reinforce distancing. This negative tape which pushes others away makes loneliness a natural consequence.

When you're in that bag you feel lonely whether you are by yourself or with a host of others. If you don't like yourself, being alone foists you into the company of the "Me-I-Can't-Stand."

You'll know you have befriended yourself when you enjoy and look forward to periodic time with your all-oneness. In fact, you will feel deprived if you take too little of this time. You'll relish private time with You just as you would with any special friend.

You'd like to take a walk or go to a movie one evening but no one you know is available? You can sit home feeling deprived or you can say to yourself, "Come on, honey, I'll go with you." Try

---

* I am indebted to Al Ross for this definition.

grabbing yourself by the hand occasionally and giving yourself your inner companionship.

Spread yourself around

All of us need the support system of friends periodically. You give yourself that gift by getting involved with formal or informal groups or individuals that are supportive. A few who see the gold in you give you the "food" that feeds. Their affirmation sustains you during the dry periods. They help you feel less threatened by those who are out to improve you. Give yourself permission to move out to Affirmers. If you feel shy, it is easy to wait for others to come to you. Most people are just as interested in having friends as you are. Instead of waiting for an invitation, extend one.

Beware of putting all your eggs in one or two baskets. Develop a circle of friends. Notice whether you choose friends on the basis of misery loves company. Notice whether you choose those worse off than you so that you can feel superior. In seeking relationships do you look for total acceptance or relationships where the other is your duplicate?

Avoid idealizing friendship. All human relationships have positives and negatives. Every person has abrasive points. Protect yourself against others' weaknesses and enjoy their positives.

Paul and Sue may be your confidants; Jane, Joe and Jill your sporting buddies; Harry, Diane and Pris are the ones who love movies and dining out; Bob, Dick and Jean may be intellectual friends; Harry, Pete and Babs may bring the fun of hashing over shop talk; Ted and Alice may share your joy in exploring or art.

The idea is to avoid limiting yourself to too few friends and expecting them to fill the many facets of You.

To use friends is to lose friends.

Each new friend is a double gift—one to yourself, one to the other. Everyone you meet can teach you something; you can enrich others as well.

Destructive tapes not only bring self-pain but they literally block us from constructive personal relationships. Being aware of these dynamics will hopefully motivate you even more to increase your own self-worth. It directly affects how and with whom you couple. Let's see how this works.

· TWELVE ·

MAKING COUPLESHIPS WORK

The new freedom

How you relate to others refers to how you connect with them. Once you shed the Critical Parent, once you stop feeling unlovable, once you befriend yourself, you are free to connect with others on an entirely new and more satisfying level. This holds true whether the other is friend, co-worker, lover, parent, child or mate.

Game-free relating
comes with self-affirmation.

Why? Simply because your couplings are not based on pain-producing deficiency needs.

The lower your self-worth, the more needy your Inner Child. And then the more likely love will be seen as something you must *get* from others. The less likely love will be shared affirmation. "I am unlovable" wipes out the possibility of "I-Thou." Others cannot enjoy you, you cannot enjoy others when you continually look through the eyes, talk with the "I's," of blame and pain.

Let's see how clinging to deficiency needs affects coupling. And then let's look at ways to couple constructively.

Round me out

Opposites attract. How clearly we see this in friendships and marriages.

The outgoing are attracted to the shy, the assertive to the passive, the strong to the weak, the confronter to the non-confronter. It is as if we say to the other, "Let me mesh with you so that together we form the whole range of human traits." Merging seems so much easier than becoming whole in our own right. Unconsciously we often attach ourselves to someone who plugs up our deficiencies. As one client put it, "I came to see that the marbles in his head fit the holes in mine."

"Loving" the other for the qualities we have failed to develop, selecting a counterpart to fill in our gaps often spells trouble. It creates dependency. And that inevitably leads to hostility. While the Child-in-us says, "I need you," that same Inner Child says, "I resent the needingness."

To repeat, the very nature of the Inner Child means it does not want to grow up. It prefers the known of the familiar; it is threatened by change. Yet to grow up is to change, to give up childhood dependencies.

Many couples have such a relationship, are aware of it and wouldn't want it any other way. No problem. The only difficulty would be if the mate leaves or dies. Then the remaining one will need to find a similar match or learn to develop those potentials that have lain dormant in the relationship.

The rounding-out qualities that initially appeal to us in the other may soon irritate and allow our destructive programming to surface.

Strait-laced, serious Jeff married his opposite—free-spirited, childlike Sue. He found her playful impulsiveness utterly appealing. A few years later he experienced these same qualities as irresponsibility and saw her as extremely undependable. The relationship deteriorated into his playing Critical Parent with her playing Not-OK Child—tapes both were unconsciously comfortable with.

Hesitant Terry cherished Barbara's outspoken definiteness. But this quality increasingly bugged him as he began to feel it as hard-to-confront domination. Yet dependency begs for dominance. And until Terry chooses to stand on his own two feet he will be drawn to dominant partners and friends.

Star-satellite, strong-weak relationships so often cause pain by their very nature. Yet look at the number of couplings built on this structure.

It is only as you and I assume the responsibility for filling our own gaps, for developing the full range of our dormant potentials that we relate out of wholeness. Such couplings spare us untold pain.

The stresses that come with a parasitic attachment do, of course, keep your Criticizer and Deprived Child content.

To see if you play Round-Me-Out, ask yourself these questions:

> What kind of partner or friend do I consciously prefer?
> What kind of partner or friend do I attract (unconscious preference)?
> What do I gain by being attracted to this type?
> What does the type I attract say about the image I project?
> What does the type I attract say about my needs?
> Am I the same with this type person as I am with others?
> What parts of me do I hold back to be with this person?
> What do I think would happen if I didn't hold back these parts?
> What do I avoid by being in this coupling?
> Would I like to be on the receiving end of what I dish out?

Blaming life or luck or chemistry for whom we attract is to avoid looking at our own unconscious choices based on deficiency needs.

Sue unconsciously attracted irresponsible men whom she could mother. It helped her deny her own need to be dependent. It kept her from facing her fear of being controlled as she had been in her childhood when she truly was dependent. Not until she worked through her early fear of helplessness was she attracted to independent men who could give as well as receive. Rounding herself out was the solution to avoiding a parasitic arrangement.

When we fall "out of love" with our other half we can rush to seek a duplicate. Or we can use that crisis as an opportunity to become whole in our own right. It is the moment of the greatest chance for growth. Then we can enjoy the others as they are rather than for how we expect them to be to make us feel whole.

Much as we may not want to face it, then, we tend to choose friends, partners and mates on the basis of psychological needs.

Coupling with the denier

With basically warm and supportive childhood family relationships, you will likely pick a mate who provides a similar climate. If, on the other hand, someone important in your childhood denied you acceptance, you will have an unconscious tendency to gravitate toward

A person like the one failing to confirm your lovability.

It may have been either of your parents (whoever took care of you), a brother, sister or another significant person in your life.

Why team up with someone likely to give you more of the same? It doesn't make sense. Not to your Adult. But it is rarely your Adult that "falls in love." It is your Deprived Child that experiences "falling in love" because it wants to fall into the deprivation-climate of the past. This is an unconscious process, but allows us to keep the same amount of emotional distance we're used to. Or to play out the original family drama.

It's as if the Not-OK Child reasons, "I'll pick one like the rejector so I can keep on trying to make the grade. But I'll (unconsciously) choose one I know I'll lose with. That guarantees me the safety of the known." The great double bind.

Should your mate not come through with the "right" blend of discounts, distancing or domination, you (unconsciously again) act out until the other obliges. *Whoever you did not make it with in childhood then is apt to be the type the Child-in-you "falls in love*" *with*. It needed their validation to cement its lovability. But since it believes it is unlovable, it seeks one allowing it to hold on to its negative Self Belief System. And your Inner Child will do everything in its power to see that the other goes along with the plot.

Who marries whom at the wedding altar? Often it's two whose Not-OKnesses interlock. This arrangement allows the old pain to continue.

Paula had a warm, relaxed relationship with her passive father. Her mother was a critical dominator. It was not surprising that she "fell in love" with a man who would treat her as her mother had. Her husband's father was the heavy Criticizer who victimized his needing-to-be-victimized mother. Both re-created in marriage what was played out before them. His need to control and Paula's need to be controlled made them a "perfect match."

Betsy's father valued her deeply and was an active life-loving man. Her mother was a passive, dependent loner who rejected her. Both Betsy's husbands duplicated her mother's style. She was unaware that her Not-OK Child chose that type. Her disillusionment led to her rejecting marriage per se.

Bob's mother and younger brothers and sisters totally adored him. His older brother and father rejected him because of his strengths. Bob married a woman who did not value him. Her personality makeup was like that of his older brother. In marriage he continued to struggle to make it with someone who could not love him because of his assets. Just as his strengths had threatened his older brother and father, so they threatened her.

In couplings we often re-create what we left behind.

Parent-child matches

Many couplings then are basically parent-child relationships. The Parent-mate plays responsible, giving controller. The Child-mate plays taking controllee—irresponsible, rebellious or weak. But his or her willingness to give up wholeness and integrity is the price paid. Always remember the Child-mate's emotional investment is in not growing up. The Parent-mate may push on the Child-mate to grow up but often sabotages such effort. Why? If the "Child" grows up, the "Parent" is left with no job to do. And away goes the stance that has provided the Parent-mate's food allowing him or her to feel important.

Interestingly enough the Weak One is often weak only when Strong is around. Weakness is used as a copout for not doing, for not getting involved, to gain attention or to continue the game of Victim and Powerless.

Although Strong may seem to dominate, Weak—through passive resistance—actually calls the shots. Weak only has to fall flat and Strong moves in to carry the ball. An exhausting tirade from Strong may cause Weak to reluctantly move. But then Weak has the double satisfaction of pushing Strong into an upset along with getting to play Poor Me—a role that's neurotically enjoyed.

The seeming container
is often the contained.

So, father-daughter, mother-son, hawk-dove, master-slave couplings abound. The power struggle of who controls and who feeds whom (coming from destructive past tapes) is the dominant theme.

Those marriages in which both mates think they've signed an unwritten "you take care of me" contract can be in for rough sledding. Two "needy" Child tapes rarely match. And much of the jockeying is centered around "You do it" vs. "No, you do it." If neither gives in, the burden is often shifted to the children.

Trauma with game change

Static invariably results if either Parent-mate or Child-mate tries to change the relationship. The original basis for the coupling is naturally threatened.

Paul only felt he counted when others were dependent on him. His past tapings taught that his survival depended on staying in power. He had a strong need to give but only on condition that he call the shots. Since Givers gravitate toward Takers, it was not surprising that he married Cindy, whose Inner Child had a strong need to lean on others' strengths.

Once she tired of the price that role exacted, she started to push toward developing her person strengths. She wanted more say in how she handled her life. Paul, however, was not about to give up his power. So he tried *Strategy #1*—he *increased his "goodies."* For example, he gave her a larger allowance but still insisted on monitoring how she spent it.

When Cindy resisted this control by getting a part-time job and making her own decisions for handling her money, he went to *Strategy #2*—*anger* and *strong criticism.*

Cindy stuck to her guns, so he reverted to *Strategy #3*—*abandonment.* With a defiant, "Well, have your own way and see how fast you get yourself in a mess!" he totally ignored her in every possible way and specialized in flirting with other women in her presence.

Cindy still didn't buckle; she handled both her home and job responsibilities with increasing success, consulting outsiders when she hit a snag. Paul couldn't tolerate her being able to function without him, so he dropped back to *Strategy #4*—the *great butter-up.* He tried to woo, please and cajole her back into dependency. But she refused the bait.

None of Paul's tactics were done with malice aforethought. He unwittingly went through these gyrations under the influence of his controlling Critical Parent tape—his personal survival strategy.

Because Cindy was sensitive to Paul's basic pain—fear that he was unimportant if he wasn't controlling—she wisely continued, regardless of which tactic was used, to reassure Paul about his importance to her. She quietly held her ground, kept letting him know she loved him as a person but no longer needed a father. She didn't withdraw, retaliate or run roughshod over him. She made it extremely clear that she only wanted to change the game rules as to how they related.

Gradually as Paul saw that he had even greater value to her because of his person, he guardedly moved away from needing to control so tightly. Had she been less sensitive to his real need—to be appreciated as a lovable person—or had Paul been less receptive to the advantages coming to him from her growing up, the marriage may well have ended.

The point is that changing master-slave relationships is not accomplished without stress, especially if only one of the couple wants to redistribute the power. Even when both want that, a great deal of manipulation and juggling for position goes on in the struggle to find a co-equal balance.

Why? If all you've known from your earliest days is controlling or being controlled, co-equal relating feels absolutely foreign. It's like trying to function without gravity. In this case the "gravity" is dominance or submission. Up or down. The lower your self-worth the more extensively you are into this game. So it takes time, awareness, effort and no small amount of trial and error to move a vertical position to the horizontal one of co-operation rather than competition.

Coupling by its very nature is a natural setup for triggering off old tapes.

Renegotiating original ground rules causes old programmed voices to set up a mighty roar.

The interlocking dependency of master-slave couplings automatically, of course, shuts *both* partners off from the joy of wholeness.

Some people try alternate roles. Controller divorces controllee, decides to feature Helpless Child and marries a controller. Neither alternative feels good, so marriage of course is a trap.

The trap is not marriage but the unconcious decision to let only one half of your person operate in a relationship—the decision to play "Up" or "Down." The trap is not marriage but the decision to use it to play out the past "knowns." As marriages move to co-equal partnerships—where each is free to express all facets of being and each is free of destructive tapes—much of this pain will dissolve. The good news is that couplings that allow you to stay with childhood pain can be restructured.

Co-equal relating

Co-equal does not mean "I do my thing, you do yours. We each go our separate ways and if we touch in passing, that's neat."

Rather, co-equal means "We are each persons first and foremost. Each of us wants to be affirmed, not used. Each of us wants recognition for our pluses, not criticism for our minuses. Each of us has separate unique talents that clamor to be expressed. Each of us has a unique inner world that makes personal sense. We each flourish better with the other's aware interest and caring about our inner world. We each appreciate empathic understanding for all of our feelings. We each assume the responsibility for becoming whole in our own right . . . separate yet interdependent."

Co-equal means working co-operatively as a team, each supporting the other's growth without violating the integrity of self, other or the relationship. It means developing some common interests and goals.

"How can I meet my whole person preferences while helping you satisfy yours?" is the issue for both partners. Neither has the answer for the other; each supports the partner in finding his or her own answers.

Couple A relate co-equally. His work largely supports the family financially. She assumes most of the child care and home maintenance jobs. In addition she works outside the home fifteen hours a week. However, he pitches in whether with a diaper change or vacuum when she needs help. Conversely, she may lend him a hand with mowing the lawn or washing the car when his schedule is heavy. There is a give and take.

Couple B handle their co-equal relationship differently. They both share housekeeping, child care and breadwinning duties. Each shares equal responsibility.

Couple C are co-equal along more traditional lines. He is the sole wage earner; she is the homemaker by preference. Both, however, support each other's interests. He doesn't look down on the importance of her club activities or volunteer work. Nor does he resent her occasional trips to conventions. He needs a night out "with the boys" and she a night out "with the girls." There is an atmosphere of mutual support. There is a sensitivity to when the other needs a helping hand and it is freely offered.

Co-equaling comes in a whole range of variations. But it involves mutual need-meeting. Co-operation is the key.

This delicate balance requires non-rigidity, compromise, patience, sensitivity, tolerance, compassion, awareness, hanging loose, non-possessiveness, giving, taking, sharing and a sense of fair play. Each of these ingredients feeds the flowingness and the flowering that surely result. No wonder fulfilling couplings are rare. They require two people who are open and willing to work.

Living out the Golden Rule with each other creates a psychic We that violates neither. And it is through this intimate psychic We-ness that soul-touching takes place. Not continually but at various little moments in time. Each fresh touching enriches the bond of joy in the relationship. Such a bond rarely just happens—it is nurtured and worked on.

An ideal? Yes. But it is possible when we relate from wholeness rather than deficiency.

Does co-equal mean you never take your Inner Child to your partner and ask for nurturing? Not at all. The difference is you don't freeze into the Needing Child stance as an ongoing way to relate to your mate.

On occasion Debbie's Inner Child is center stage. She is aware of it and freely says to her husband, "Right now I feel like a little four-year-old that needs comforting." And he feels free to fold her in as a father might. She asks directly for what she wants rather than trying to manipulate her husband with whining, pouting or irresponsible games. She talks straight. And she is equally comfortable about giving when her husband's Inner Child surfaces and he asks for some temporary mothering.

The "good" parent need

Interwoven with the dominance-submission struggle is each partner's hope to convert the other permanently into the "Good-Parent-I-Never-Had." "You give me what 'they' didn't," is the thrust.

When the other doesn't come through, your Deprived Child sees the other as the denier, the enemy. And so the punishing begins. Now you can sock your partner with the leftovers from the slush fund accumulated toward this troublesome parent-from-your-past.

So frequently in counseling, one partner lets out the collected anger at his or her mate. After the dumping, the counselor may ask, "Who from your past would you like to have said the same words to?" Invariably the answer is, "My mother," "My father," "My grandmother," "My brother," "My sister." Much of the flak from your partner is ammunition deflected from earlier childhood scenes.

Flailing at the parent/sibling-who-is-now-your-partner never solves the problem. Each of us needs to finish the business with the significant ones from our childhood before we are ready for co-equal coupling.

Parenting problems

The highly dependent adult has trouble parenting his or her own children. Because youngsters are dependent on us for a long period, they need to lean on our strength particularly during their early years.

If your own dependency needs are strong, parenting takes a heavy toll. It is as if you say to your youngster, "Look, I need to lean. So you don't lean on me."

If you inwardly reject your own dependency needs, a further message is communicated: "I can't stand my own dependency so I can't take yours. You're too much like me—a part of me I reject." And lash-outs or rejections occur around this point.

Child-mates and Parent-mates frequently play youngsters off against their partners, trying to get children to choose sides. Or use them to keep distance between themselves to avoid facing conflicts in the marriage.

The family is a system of interactions. Pain in any one member is felt by all.

Unknowingly we parents often enlist the total family to recon-struct the patterns from our childhood home. Harriet grew up in a family in which her brother was its official pain-bearer. He was the Bad Guy. Unconsciously she elected her son to her brother's role as the family scapegoat.

Mary watched her mother put her father down. He was the enemy. She borrowed that script and tried to alienate her children from their father. Her mother's Voice-in-her-head told her, "Men are beasts." Even though she remembered feeling sorry for her fa-ther as a child and wished she could have had a relationship with him, her mother's injunction overrode that wish.

Remember in Chapter Nine you looked at roles in your family. You checked on who the Bad Guy was in your childhood family, who was the Irresponsible One, the Clown, the Failure, the Weak-ling, the Star. Now ask yourself, "Am I unwittingly reactivating these old roles in my present family?" If so, you can consciously choose to stop, to change the drama. If necessary, a professional assist can help you avoid a repeat.

Not everyone is cut out for parenthood. It is a long-term, demanding job. Just because it brings wholehearted joy and deep meaning to some does not mean that it "should" do the same for you. Hopefully, those who do not choose parenting can be allowed that freedom without society's frown. Children need adults who want to be parents. And not all adults welcome that ongoing responsibility.

Marriage in danger

"The institution of marriage is going down the drain!" A red flag waved by the statistics, the media and our own observations. Yet no sooner do husband and wife split than most start looking for a new partner—either for marriage or live-in.

The expectation is that changing the name, the face and the place means bliss will surely follow. A short time later each discovers the new partner is quite like the past one. And the same old games come back to plague. Why? We used our first mate to put our own unresolved problems on. We then take those same problems into the new relationship.

When second marriages or couplings work out the primary reason is sweat. Each works at lowering expectations, giving up Cinderella-Prince Charming fantasies and tries to avoid things that cause trouble. The major change is an improvement in adjusting to the realities of the other and the relationship that marriage involves.

Some second couplings, of course, are more nurturing because one or the other partner has outgrown some of the old destructive tapes, matured emotionally and chosen a more mature partner the second time around.

Role expectations

"My wife and I lived together for three years before getting married. We didn't want the divorce mess our parents had. Things went so well that we decided we could make a go of marriage. But trouble started almost immediately. We can't figure out what went wrong!"

Trial marriage believers, take note.

The instant vows are exchanged each looks at the other in a new way. Instead of room-mate or lover you see husband or wife. *And all the expectations long stored in the wings of your mind as to how a mate should be or act descend.* These role expectations—collected from your parents, the media, our culture, your needs and observations—silently wait for the sound of the "I do's" before surfacing.

When both husband and wife enjoy traditional marriage roles they report a higher degree of satisfaction. Those who tire of the role or who have never identified with it experience more stress in marriage. The stress is heightened if one mate wants to stay with the roles and the other does not.

A major force disrupting the institution of marriage, of course, has been the movement away from the stereotyped husband-wife role. As you know in times past the rule was: "You play housewife-passive-nurturer. I'll play breadwinner-aggressive-invulnerable."

Technology, increasing educational and work opportunities for women, the women's liberation movement, mobility, an increasing emphasis on material comforts, smaller families, the breakdown of the family clan support system, financial pressures and the wave of humanism have each played a part in weakening this patriarchal stereotype. The ideal of togetherness during all leisure time has added to the pressures in marriage.

Modern women are asked to function in many roles: wife, mother, chauffeur, social secretary, housekeeper, cook, friend, nurse, confidante and therapist. Sometimes, in addition, they must also be breadwinners. Modern men are expected to earn a living, be a handyman, gardener, painter, mechanic, friend, father, husband, protector and therapist. If all these roles aren't your cup of tea you may feel inadequate or be told you are. Somehow, while juggling all these expectancies, you try to find time for your own person needs . . . to "actualize" your potentials.

Is it any wonder that there is a rumbling among the married troops? It's a tall order for any one person to handle adequately. And those on a perfectionist's trip often find themselves burned out in the process.

The more you evolve your own wholeness, the more you offer your mate respect and fair play, the more you put roots into community supports, the less stress you place on your marriage.

A first step in this direction is seeing your partner as a person first and foremost—outside the role of mate. A difficult but not impossible task once you see yourself in that light.

The shadow of our parents' role modeling, the myths of literature, our culture and the media lie like a great contaminating smog bank that can choke the life from the relationship unless both work consistently to brush roles aside. Role expectations cause real conflicts unless each is content with the stereotype. Today, regardless of your own feelings on the subject, fewer couples are content simply to live out roles.

Alternatives to the nuclear family and traditional marriage are, of course, being experimented with and publicized. Open marriage in terms of sex partners has been spotlighted. The testimony of Masters and Johnson as well as many marriage counselors suggests that such arrangements are *not* satisfactory in the long run. Such setups are too often used as solutions to more basic problems in relating.

Regardless of your life-style, the power of your tapes eventually makes itself felt in all your relationships. Until and unless destructive tapes are reduced, you will be drawn toward people, jobs and life-styles that cut into tranquillity. Merely changing the outer structure does not necessarily alter these tapes. That's still an inside job.

Ideal vs. real

In times past marriage was basically a contractual arrangement to increase family holdings, ensure political alliances, perpetuate family lines, or establish a work unit with all hands pitching in to perform vital tasks. Love was not even considered.

In the seventeenth century the idea of romantic and unrequited love developed. The one and only prince rescued the pining damsel. And you know how the fantasy ended. If they got together at all, it was for "happily ever after."

Some three hundred years later we are still idealizing romantic love. These legends of romantic love join our own unfulfilled childhood wants to form the ideal we look for. The ideal mate is seen as the custodian for making dreams come true. The highly romantic prefer life in the clouds to life on earth. Romance has long been the ideal; marriage the real. As one bumper sticker put it, "If love is a dream, marriage is an alarm clock."

Too many of us marry an image—a stock character spun out of our fantasies and needs—not a real person. And we are disappointed when reality hits. We find that real mates belch, snore, have body odors, get grouchy and are not preoccupied with always being available and forever understanding us. They have their own needs and problems. Real people are real people; not role-players or image-protectors.

Have you ever thought this about your mate? "You're not the person I married." Of course not. You have bumped against the other's reality and your image has been shattered. But wouldn't this happen with almost anyone you lived with daily?

In idealizing
you set yourself up for disappointment.

"You're not the same person" implies the other agreed not to change. Impossible. The growth process is relentless; change and psychological movement are inevitable. Some of us move toward increasing wholeness. Some spiral down into increasing pain.

Massive evidence has been collected over the years about the "ages and stages" of childhood development. We have found that there are predictable behaviors that accompany growth. Only recently have researchers found that such stages do not cease with age twenty-one. Gail Sheehy's book *Passages* discusses the accumulated evidence of the predictable crises that take place in adulthood.

Periodically most of us stop for life reviews. That is, we reshift our self-statements, re-evaluate and reorganize our attitudes, priorities, values and goals.

Those searching for Mr. or Ms. Right look for someone to

fulfill their ideals;
be perfect;
fill their holes;
help them re-establish past climates;
meet all their needs;

hold on to their "Imperfect Me";
remain stationary;
avoid intimacy and risk.

This is not what true love is all about. But far too often this dynamic masquerades as love.

Take a moment to check your expectancies.

What were your original expectations for a mate?
What needs in you did such expectations satisfy?
Were your expectations realistic?
Did they pan out?
If you are or have been married, what are your expectations today?
Are they realistic?
What were your role expectations for yourself and your partner? What are they today?
How much are you trying to change your mate?
How much are you assuming the responsibility for your own growth?

Write out your answers and share them with your mate. (Sharing only clarifies if no put-downs are involved.) List the things you like about living with your partner; the things you dislike. How closely do these lists of likes and dislikes match your own "should" list? How do you think you come across as a person to live with? Would you like to be married to you?

Before throwing out the institution of marriage, we need to ask, "Is it the institution itself that is out of whack?" "Is it the unrealistic expectations and fantasies we dump on this relationship?" "Do past destructive tapes doom many to unhappy couplings regardless of whether marriage is involved?"

The affair

If one partner grows restless and pushes for more mature, game-free relating while the other does not, as we've seen, stresses build up. Games, of course, require two to play. Often as one stops his or her part in the game the other will, after much static, give it up. The seven-year itch frequently signals that one wants a shift from the original pattern. Without open communication and a mutual willingness to change the destructive games, however, the fourteen-year ditch may result.

Sometimes splitting up is too scary, so an affair is the choice. Basically an affair is a way to avoid dealing with the problems in the relationship. Instead of confronting and fighting for what you want, you seek an outside lover. Then nothing comes to a head.

Implicit in every affair is the fear of closeness, commitment, change or confrontation.

As long as the affair lasts, the lover is seen as the Good One, the partner as the Bad One. And you can live with the Child fantasy of the angel who gives and the ogre who withholds. You don't have to deal with the reality of the blends.

Reinforcing the affair is our culture's emphasis on disposability and instant gratification. Use 'em up. Toss 'em out. Instant flip to one more satisfying at the moment. Natural resources, tissues, soft drink bottles, cars, relationships. Use them according to your needs. Dispose of them when they no longer serve your purpose. "Have it now, face the consequences later" pervades.

In the long run we reap what we sow. There is no way to avoid the consequences of our acts. One way or another all concerned eventually pay the price. This is a law of life and not simply a moral preaching.

You may be a person who operates most comfortably with no-strings attachments and limited commitments. It may sound harsh but from a psychological point of view these setups save you from looking within and dealing with early hurts and decisions regarding sustained intimacy. They spare you the struggle of hammering out the challenges that sustained relating involves. And that requires a lot of energy.

Energy is, in a way, like money. You may not choose to spend yours on working at deep, ongoing commitments. Each of us is free to make this choice. Flitting is for some, committing is for others. A price is exacted for either choice. Just be aware of both the short-

and long-range costs to yourself and others when you make your choice. Alerting your partner of your stance (regardless of which it is) is part of fair play.

The human being seems to need an ongoing support system. Through the ages the family has been one such support system, first for physical survival and later for psychological enhancement. In countries where governments have tried to break down the institution of the family there has not yet been evidence that this produced greater inner peace. Indeed, when restrictions have been lifted there has been a pulling back to family groups.

Fully functioning humans are social creatures. We seek social interaction and social groups that feed belongingness. Various facets of our person are brought more fully into being by interacting. And a sense of rootedness as a contributing member of a cohesive group builds the conviction "I count." High self-esteemers, not being afraid of closeness, prefer commitment to non-commitment. But as we've mentioned, their relationships are not characterized by deficiency manipulations. Rather they tend toward supportive affirmations.

Changing parent-child matches

The paradox is that in so many couplings

**The partner has the potential
to give what is needed
when both are ready to grow up.**

"Growing up" literally involves a special kind of "divorce." A positive one. It means

divorcing yourself from the decision to replay automatically the Internal Criticizer and Not-OK tapes;

divorcing yourself from old dependencies, pain games and manipulations—the unfinished business with your parents;

divorcing yourself from no longer appropriate survival roles;

divorcing yourself from Inner Child illusions and unrealistic romantic ideals;

divorcing yourself from that most popular of all couples'
games, "if-it-weren't-for-you."

Growing up
means
growing free inside.

Trying to shape the other up is a sure-fire way to avoid looking at
ourselves, at what we do to re-create pain, at how we box ourselves
and the other in. We're far too eager to look at what the other does
that's troublesome rather than search for our part in the stress. The
Child-in-us wishes for the Fairy Godmother to turn the Difficult
One into a prince or princess. Once again, it's that Child-in-us that
wants to duck responsibility for its part in the pain.

How do you go about changing your pain-producing role expectations and tapes in your coupling?

You follow precisely the same formula for freeing yourself from
painful expectations and tapes. Remember, the first step is
awareness. You need to take the observer's position with yourself.
Take the self-inventory questions listed in this chapter under the
earlier section, *Ideal vs. real*. And you need to observe your reactions scrupulously.

Ask yourself, "Why am I having this feeling? What expectation is
it tied to? In what ways am I trying to push the other into fitting
my images, "should's" and "ought's"? In what ways is the De-
mander/Child-in-me trying to manipulate the other?"

Then you need to muster your *courage,* make a *decision* to release
the pain-producers and *act* on that decision daily. You need to
remind yourself continually to get off the other's case and get on
your own. You need to stay in close contact with your Adult's
inputs as to what is reality both in life and for this other with whom
you are coupled.

You may need to remind yourself daily of St. Francis of Assisi's
serenity prayer: "Grant me the serenity to accept the things I cannot change (namely others' attitudes and behavior), the courage to
change the things I can (specifically my attitudes and behavior),

and the wisdom to know the difference (my Adult reality orienta-
tion)."

When Jane gave up taking over for her husband, he moved in to
handle things himself. His way was different from hers but the job
got done.

When Ted quit boxing his wife in with put-downs, she began to
blossom by letting some of her real abilities emerge.

When Maxine became her own Nurturing Parent, she stopped
asking her husband, friends and children to do the job.

To repeat, awareness, honesty in looking at your own destructive
tapes, willingness to change, courage and work are all needed. But
the rewards are worth the effort to everyone except your Pain-lov-
ing Child.

Release

Remember we talked earlier about our destructive tapes being
hooked into the love of power.

The opposite of power held is release. Releasing the other to take
his or her own path is part of the power of love. Love is not manag-
ing. In fact,

**A major step
in improving coupleships
is release.**

It cannot be emphasized too strongly that the greatest barrier to
letting go is simply the Inner Dependent Child who does *not* want
to say,

"I will be whole in my own right!"

To some extent most of us at the gut level resist wholeness. We
may not think we do. But, like Tom Sawyer, we'd rather have
someone else do our fence painting while we sit back and supervise.
The easy way out, however, eases us out of joy. The central challenge of life is to grow up and develop our undeveloped attributes
and qualities. Yet we resist completeness with all the creativity at
our command.

Until we release, however, we cannot become complete. Real release may need to be a daily work process for a long time.

Sandy found all her relationships changing when she practiced the power of release.

"My counselor told me nothing short of my older sister's therapy or personal growth could ever allow her to accept me. Somehow something clicked. I wasn't a child with one sister any more. I realized I had all kinds of psychological sisters in friends. Crazy thing. Once I stopped trying to win her acceptance, I automatically could honestly accept her as she was. I stopped trying to change her to be like me. I could enjoy certain qualities she has and be completely unaffected by the things I didn't like. Guess what? Now we're very close—but not in a needing way—good friends without unreal demands and expectations. I can finally accept the ways she is different from me without judging them.

"Suddenly it hit me that I had married a guy like my sis. He has the same way of handling life. I saw I'd been doing exactly the same thing to him for twenty years that I'd done to her. I tried to get him to live life like me. I wanted him to meet my needs, to relate to me as I wanted. I tried to get him to love me as I defined love. Our marriage absolutely flipped from a roller coaster ride to smooth sailing. It's unbelievable how blind I was. I couldn't release him until I stopped needing him to change, until I started liking me. Now we have fun together and when his way differs from mine, I remind myself, 'That's his way.' And I feel so little need to change him. Apparently he felt my release because he's so much more loving. And he's changed a lot on his own. At last we seem to be friends."

Only when we *release* ourselves and others are the dormant positive potentials given a chance to awaken in coupling.

Freedom to reveal

Open communication lies at the heart of nurturing relationships. What kind of talk goes on between you and yours? Is it solely a rehash of events—a news report of the day with a bit of editorializing thrown in? Is yours a head trip coupling? Does your talk remain at the computer printout level?

Many women and certainly the vast majority of our work-oriented American men have been brainwashed against revealing feelings. Head-talk-only relationships are most apt to work out if both partners prefer that arrangement. Even so, loneliness in the relationship may be the price.

Open sharing of feelings does not mean banging on the other to give what he or she cannot give. It is appreciating and accepting what the other can give. Be aware, however, that

Psychological intimacy is not possible without appropriate sharing of feelings.

Sharing doesn't mean replaying a never-ending "Ain't it/they awful" or "Poor Me" tape.

Openness does not mean dumping on others. It does mean letting the other know how you experience your world, what's in your secret heart. This means taking the responsibility for your own feelings. "You" followed by blaming, critical, fault-finding words closes the door on nurturing coupling. It puts the responsibility on the other. It blasts self esteem. "I" followed by your inner experience reveals you to the other. Notice the difference below:

Shut-out Talk*: (Critical)	Revealing-you Talk: (Nurturing)
You watch too much TV.	I feel hungry for some of your attention.
Why don't you ever pick up after yourself?	I don't want to pick up your things. I feel I have enough to do.
Quit nagging.	I feel pushed and put down. I want more space.
Worrying will get you no-where!	I wish you didn't feel so concerned but I know that's where you are right now.

* Chapter Nine in my earlier book, *Your Child's Self-Esteem,* goes into greater detail on this all-important topic.

Revealing your feelings and wants while allowing the other to "own" his feelings and wants helps nurturing dialogue flourish. When openness is met with empathic, non-judgmental understanding, it is encouraged. Openness grows when you give the other the space to experience in his or her own unique way. Neither partner uses openness to manipulate, produce guilt or victimize the other. Feelings are simply *stated* and *received* as, "This is how it is for me right now."

Loving means caring. If you care, you care about what the other experiences. But you cannot translate that caring if the other refuses to let you in or if you refuse to let the other in. Openness is a two-way street.

Risk-taking

Implicit in openness is the willingness to risk. As we've seen, the problem is that we

Are attracted to people
who help us stay stuck on old tapes.

Then should we open up they help us reverse by being critical or pulling back. Improving relationships is easier if both have a commitment to hang in and risk growing free. It's amazing how many are frightened of real freedom . . . wholeness.

Lately, great emphasis has been placed on openness for its own sake. "Let it all hang out," we are advised. *A strong note of caution needs to be sounded.*

Openness without appropriate responsibility (checking it through your Adult tape) is strictly Impulsive Child. While impulsiveness (appropriately used) adds spice and zest to life, it can hurt you and others if its urges are relied on exclusively. High self-esteemers are responsibly impulsive.

Mary claimed Brownie points for her "honesty" by telling her husband, "I went to bed with your best friend last night and *he* really turned me on."

No amount of "honesty" sugar coating makes this anything but a blow.

More honest and responsible openness would be, "I'm deeply troubled as to why I turn myself off when we have sex. I think it's because I feel so much distance between us." Here she reveals her inner world without attacking. Such sharing opens up the possibility for a mutual dialogue so that the problem can be worked on constructively.

If the basic feeling behind her first blast was, "I really want to hurt you," it is far more appropriate to share that feeling rather than act on it by delivering the verbal blow.

Temper openness with responsibility to Self and others.

We all need to ask ourselves:

What are the risks if I choose to reveal certain feelings?
What are the risks if I choose *not* to reveal certain feelings?
Do I open up only to those likely to reject my sharing?
Is my openness only a cover for attack or blame?

When you answer these questions, ask yourself which "I" responds. Is it your Scared/Rebellious Child "I"? Is it the Critical Parent "I"? Is it your Adult "I"?

If you have been increasing your self-worth by the steps we've discussed, you are more likely to assume the courage to risk closeness. You don't fear you'll disappear or drop dead if you reveal your vulnerability. And, to repeat, your own self-acceptance makes you less vulnerable. Surely hurts will come. But you don't see them as ghastly catastrophes. You experience them out. And you know

No pain no gain.

Different intimacy tolerances

A second caution is important. When you work toward increasing psychological intimacy between you and your partner, be aware that you and the other will probably have different tolerance levels for how long, how intense and how often those soul-touching moments are.

Marie, like many women in our culture, was in touch with a great number of her feelings and able to share a few sporadically. Her husband was not nearly so aware of his and could tolerate feeling talk for only brief moments. She became involved in some personal growth groups. In that safety she opened up increasingly. She experienced the warmth of closeness to others as they openly shared.

"It was like I saw what was possible in the group," said Marie, "and I became very frustrated with my husband. I moved from 20 per cent sharing to 40 per cent. As a result of my movement, he slowly moved from 1 per cent to 20 percent. But there is still this big gap."

He matched her growth percentagewise, but he started from a more closed position originally. Banging on him to take giant leaps could cause him to withdraw. Enjoying the 20 per cent intimate talk he could give at that time and getting her remaining 20 per cent need met with other friends would leave neither unsatisfied.

Expecting to have sustained intimacy talk with the person you live with on a twenty-four-hour basis is not realistic. We all differ in our tolerance levels. And our growth needs to be measured from our starting point. Recognizing your own and your partner's limitations is part of love and acceptance.

Inventory time

Here is a list of questions to check out your handling of relationships. If you can truthfully answer "No" to all of them, you are probably holding up your half of the coupleship constructively. Those that may still apply to you are simply areas for further growth. As you go over them, be brutally honest with yourself. It is amazing how easy it is for all of us to see ourselves through rose-colored glasses.

Am I trying to push my partner to be my good parent?
Am I trying to work out my unfinished childhood business
  through my mate?

Do I push on the other to be that troublesome parent or sibling from my past?

Do I expect the other to do all the giving? To make nice for me?

Do I expect the other to carry most of the responsibility? Do I shoulder at least half the load?

Do I avoid closeness by refusing to reveal my inner experiencing world?

Do I push the other to meet my preconceived expectations and role needs?

Am I asking the other to round me out?

Do I keep my eye on the other to watch for what he or she does to cause conflict?

Do I consistently push the other's sensitive buttons?

Do I lock horns just to prove I'm right?

Do I insist on always doing my own thing regardless of the other's preferences? Or go along with some of them but pout all the way?

Do I choose not to risk? Do I get back at the other by attacking or passive resistance?

A basic question to ask yourself is:

What actions, attitudes, decisions or survival tactics of mine keep my problems alive?

Honest soul-searching and a commitment to self-responsibility are more likely to pay off than the quickie divorce or a series of affairs.

Getting started

After you and your partner have finished an honest self-inventory, get together with a mutual agreement that you'll dialogue off these ten basic guidelines:

1. I assume you are a lovable and valuable person. I assume I am a lovable and valuable person. (If this is a difficult assumption,

skip ahead to the last chapter, reread the foregoing chapters. Remind yourselves that each of you is separate from your behavior. Remind yourselves that how you or the other behaved in the past was done without present awareness.)

2. I assume that your inner world makes sense to you. I know my inner world makes sense to me.

3. To some degree you and I have been *unconsciously* relating automatically off old negative tapings. This does not mean you or I are "bad" but merely that we've been unaware.

4. Take each inventory question, one at a time, and share with your partner what your self-searching has revealed to you about what you may have been doing in the partnership that caused stress. (Here each takes responsibility for him or herself.) The idea is that you each talk about *only* what you see yourself doing. You do not take the other person's inventory. You share only the findings of your own. What old tapes are being triggered, what old survival games have you been re-enacting? What old vulnerabilities are being touched; whose lines from the past are you falling back on?

(Often, one of you may be more open to looking within than the other. It will be tempting to "help" the other see his or her games. Resist this for the simple reason that it doesn't work. Know that the one who is more open will be in a better position to grow. Each of us can only grow in his or her own way and own time. Growth cannot be forced. Rarely, if ever, do both grow at the same rate. If I stop looking at me because you won't look at you, I only impede my own growth).

5. In this dialogue each agrees *only to listen* to the other. Any remarks like, "Well, I've wondered when you'd see that," or, "I've tried to tell you that for years," or any body language that sends judgment, disinterest, or non-caring kills open dialogue in short order. Make a mutual agreement that neither will use any shared input as later ammunition against the other. This is crucial.

(It's hard enough for some of us to look within; it's even harder to risk sharing. When we do, we put our tenderness and vulnerability on the line. The whole rationale behind all our games has been basically a brave attempt to protect that vulnerability. We each need safety and caring if we are to feel encouraged to open up.)

6. The purpose of sharing is not to dump guilt on yourself but rather to share *objective data* with the other. It's as if you stand outside yourself and comment on your observations. For example, "I notice that I really get bossy, especially when I'm feeling unneeded. I've tried to figure out why and I think it's because I've got this big need to feel important when I play Camp Fire Director."

7. Remember your first go-round on a self-inventory may reveal only certain patterns to you. Tomorrow or next week if you are committed to ongoing inventory-taking, new awarenesses will dawn.

8. After sharing your awareness, make a contract with yourself and your partner to avoid your pitfall. *Build a plan of action.* This means you will look for other ways to relate or handle your life. "What other options are available to me?" is the focus. In the Camp Fire Director game mentioned in 6. above, you might decide, "When I start feeling anxious and unimportant, I feel it would work out better just to share that feeling with you rather than act in a way that makes us both unhappy."

9. No matter how dedicated you are to your new choice, years of habit and the safety of the known make slipping back a strong possibility, especially during times of stress. When you revert, just be aware, recommit but refuse to put yourself down for it. If the behavior is continual and destructive, get professional help.

(Remember, all growth proceeds by fits and starts; trees don't grow overnight. The two of you can erase the old game lines and redo the interaction along new lines. It's awkward at first. But with continued practice the new ways become spontaneous.)

10. To repeat, if you bog down despite your efforts, get outside help. Otherwise, these same self-defeating games will continue to plague or will be played out in any new relationship.

Having looked at couplings in general, let's consider a few additional specific issues.

· THIRTEEN ·

ISSUES IN COUPLING

Sex

Bad relationship, bad sex. This dynamic is not always true but for a great many it is.

Contrary to popular belief, sex starts in the head. However, an unsatisfying sex life is easier to focus on as *the* problem rather than looking at some of the dynamics we've already talked about. Many times opening up lines of communication between the couple, readjusting expectations and cleaning out the slush fund of accumulated anger toward both parent figures and your partner clears up the sexual impasse.

On the other hand, if your Critical Parent tape is on, you drag your "should's," unrealistic expectations and judgments into bed with you. Its negative attitudes are loaded with injunctions that prevent satisfaction. It is crucial to check out your conditioning. Do any of these fit what your Inner Criticizer believes?

Touching body parts is bad; body pleasure is wrong; sensuality is animalistic; the genitals are dirty or are organs to be ashamed of; sex is something to be endured; sex is something "nice" people don't enjoy; don't look, act or feel sexy; elimination of body waste materials is dirty; sexual secretions are evil; using sex to hurt others is OK; withholding sex from the partner you have a commitment to is a good way to get even; something is wrong with you if you don't experience an orgasm with every sexual act; don't have an orgasm; don't enjoy foreplay; don't bother to facilitate your partner to a climax; only men should be sexually aggressive; performance is what counts; don't let go—the list goes on and on.

The point is that you may have bought attitudes that cut into the full enjoyment of your sensuality and your sexuality. If so, you have been taught to disown an important part of yourself.

All kinds of marriage and sex manuals abound. Many are largely concerned with the mechanics and giving you permission to use them. But unless the tapes that interfere with body pleasuring are dealt with they may be of little use to you. Many of the attitudes you bought were subtle, non-verbal cues given off by your parents, agemates, the media and our culture. And they carry as much if not more weight than the verbal messages you received. The low self-esteemer characteristically believes he or she does not deserve to be pleasured.

On the other hand so much emphasis has lately been placed on the sex act that sexual pleasure is for some a strictly demanded right. If orgasms (or multiple ones) aren't reached every time, today's brainwashed couple may blame themselves or each other. Sometimes is not enough. The expectation then is that the marriage bed is an arena for nightly Olympics. Hardly realistic. Such expectations and performance demands make the ideal even less likely.

Some of you have suffered sexual trauma in the past. Its impact has left you fearful of or with a profound distaste for sex. You cheat yourself and your relationships by choosing not to get competent help to work such feelings through.

Others of you may fear to give yourself permission to enjoy your sexuality, fantasizing you might go hog-wild. You can let all these feelings into your awareness and still remain responsible to yourself and others. You have only to choose to stay in close contact with your Adult tape. You are not a pawn to total Child impulsivity unless you choose to be. To repeat, the choice is always yours.

The partner disinterested in sex may actually be rebelling against sex with a stranger. When the other is unknown to us out of the bed, there is no bond of psychological closeness to respond to physically. Hiding behind defenses and pretense for fear of being possibly hurt or possessed cuts off sexual spontaneity and the open giving of each to the other. The Controller has problems with relaxing and simply letting go. The Withdrawer fears letting the other make inner contact.

Uncommitted sex is a plastic substitute for psychological intimacy —closeness. Alienation and loneliness are not erased by physical acts. When skill in techniques is wedded to love, mutual respect, shared values and tender caring commitment, you experience an unbelievably deep intimacy that enriches both lives.

Nurturing permissions

The Nurturing Parent Voice gives you full permission to enjoy and relish your total physical body including its sexual and sensual feelings. It does not cast the pall of shame, guilt, evil or performance over the miracle of the sexual process. Solid contact with your Adult tape keeps you from using sex to exploit others or yourself. You experience all your sexual feelings in all their varying nuances as normal and healthy. But you do not act on them irresponsibly. You do not equate sex per se with love. Rather you see the intimacy of sexual enjoyment as one of the many ways you communicate love to the partner of your commitment.

High self-esteemers enjoy responsibly handled sex. But they do not blow it out of proportion as the be-all of life. Nor do they underestimate its importance and joy. Like all other life experiences, they see it in proportion.

Just as with your expectations for marriage, so your expectations for sex need to be checked out. Ask yourself whether your attitudes toward love, sex and commitment come from your Critical or your Nurturing tapes. If they come from the former, you can choose to let them go. If you are not willing to release them, press yourself for what your payoffs are for clinging to them. Some part in you benefits and it is usually your Sad/Bad/Scared Kid or your Critical Parent. Ask yourself how much longer you want these Voices to rule your life.

Commitment in coupling

An increasing number believe it is impossible to be committed to another while remaining true to yourself. They see the two as mutually exclusive.

If you're filled with negative taping you now know that your relationships involve manipulations, dominance-submission or win-lose arrangements. Then commitment means some form of capitulation. It smacks of obligation and loss of autonomy.

The word commitment means to connect—to entrust. True commitment is difficult unless you know who You truly are and have a willingness to connect and entrust your Self-affirming inner world with another's.

For the negatively taped the great fear behind committing is the fear of vulnerability, the fear of openly exposing yourself, the fear that the other will use your vulnerability to his or her advantage. To your disadvantage.

A second great fear is that if you openly connect with another and allow the other to entrust himself or herself to you, you have a commitment to live up to that trust.

You know that the Adult-in-you is aware of the consequences of behavior and acts accordingly. If you play life as the Impulsive Child then you pretend (turn off the Adult Voice) that you are not responsible for your acts. This is pure fantasy. For those who do not want to face this reality, commitment is to be avoided.

True commitment is based on mutual trust. It is only for those willing to embrace the Adult part of their personality. Nurturing Adult commitment says, "I openly connect with you. You can openly trust connecting with me. We will jointly avoid using our mutual vulnerability for self-serving purposes." Since so many of us have had our vulnerability trampled on and used, it is not surprising that commitment looks dangerous.

Love involves sharing and risking the closeness of the Whole Me with the Whole You. It is not trying to shape you up to fit my images nor do my job or my parents' job for me. It is enjoying in spite of imperfection. Love is seeing the diamond through the dust.

Since using is not an issue, love's commitment means each gives the Self and the other the freedom to be. Each is open to and cares about the other. Neither uses freedom as license. Each is committed to growth. Mutuality is the key.

Broken relationships

If you lose a loved one through death, divorce or separation, you go through a grieving process, even those of you who might actually be glad to be free of the former relationship.

When you love someone—or have needed them—bonds of attachment are formed regardless of how satisfactory or unsatisfactory that relationship has been. When those bonds are broken you actually suffer a double loss: the loss of the attachment figure and the loss of a role. Not only has the person departed from your life but the widowed or divorced have lost the role of husband or wife. In a sense you sink emotional roots into the soil of that bonding and now you are uprooted. Naturally the Child-in-you grieves.

Stages of grief

When grief strikes it is as if our bodies protect us at first with a kind of numbness. "It can't be true," "It isn't really happening" pads us against the shock of reality.

Then the feeling of abandonment—the feeling of emotional separation, loneliness and helplessness—hits. And old tender spots from childhood are triggered off.

All of us have experienced some degree of abandonment as children.

> Our parents left us with a relative, sitter or teacher and we were too young to realize they'd return.
>
> Our parents, teachers or friends did not understand our feelings and we felt abandoned to handle them by ourselves.
>
> A brother, sister or playmate wouldn't play with us or ran off, and we felt deserted.

Some group did not include us and we felt excluded and lonely.

We were frightened of the dark or were put in a hospital and felt abandoned again.

A pet died or ran away; a beloved toy broke, was lost or given away; an important person in our lives left or died. Each situation gave us experience with loss. And helplessness was triggered off.

Although all of us have collected varying degrees of temporary or permanent loss, some have larger backlogs of abandonment feelings than others. Regardless, death, divorce and separation trigger off the lonely, helpless Child feelings accumulated from the past.

A third feeling of anger and rage invariably comes with significant loss. Even when the relationship was broken by death, the Child-in-you consciously or unconsciously rages, "How could you do this to me?" If you are divorced or separated you often find it easier than the widowed to get in touch with your anger over the parting. The one who made the break often rants, "If only you had been different I wouldn't have to suffer this uprooting." The one left fumes, "How could you desert me after all I've done for you?" If ever there is a tendency to put your eye on the other, it is in this situation. The Criticizer and Helpless Voices alternately dominate the stage.

Mixed in may come a large measure of other assorted emotions:

guilt because of the anger, which often results in apathy or depression; confusion and bewilderment over what went wrong;

a constant rehash of events and self-questioning to find the cause;

a weeping for the lost pleasant moments;

wistfulness for what might have been;

feelings of failure with consequent loss of self-esteem;

fear of ever investing emotionally in another relationship;

anxiety over possible financial pressures, changes in life-style and the effects on the children involved.

To say this is a time of strong and volatile feelings for most is putting it mildly. Wide mood swings, impulsivity, accident-proneness, feeling immobilized and a general lessened ability to make rational decisions and work effectively flood in.

With so much going on emotionally it is not surprising that you feel tense, restless and have trouble eating and sleeping. Those having formed attachments to food, drugs or alcohol are apt to turn to them more heavily for solace. For some there is frantic searching behavior—a need to attach quickly to some rock in the storm. For others there is a needful turning to work, church and friends to shore up a self-support system.

If none of this fits for you, it may simply mean that you had a marriage but never invested in it emotionally. Or your tapes have taught you to deny feelings. Possibly your abandonment slush fund had relatively little in it. On the other hand, you may have gradually divorced your mate emotionally long before the literal separation or death took place. For you the split largely meant stepping away from an already dead relationship or old hassles.

Sometimes in marriage there is a series of temporary separations before the final one. Apart each tends to remember the positives; once together the old abrasive games are reactivated. (As an aside, it is almost always best to get marriage counseling help after a reconciliation to prevent a repeat of what caused the split.)

For the widowed there is a tendency to comfort oneself with pleasant memories of the deceased, to forget his or her abrasive points. Comparing the departed idealized one with new dates is apt to be part of keeping him or her alive in memory and avoiding a possible future attachment that the Inner Child reasons could bring another such loss.

Effects on the larger clan

Questions of loyalty and how to maintain which clan relationships invariably surface after divorce. The outside members' attitudes toward husband and wife, the choosing of sides, the effect on the couple's friends and relatives are all thorny issues.

The temptation of each mate to put the other down in their children's eyes is strong as it helps reduce tension to have someone on your side. One or both may subtly or directly grill the children as to what the other is saying and doing. Children are almost invariably caught in between with divided loyalties. They truly need to be spared the role of "go-between" as they have all of their own feelings to handle. And that's a big enough job.

Avoid scolding yourself if you are tempted to involve them, but avoid acting that temptation out.

The parent with visitation rights often unconsciously plays Mr. or Ms. Santa Claus, showering the youngsters with goodies and throwing out all limits on behavior for the brief time they are together. The parent with custody usually feels frustrated and disadvantaged because she or he cannot chalk up such popularity points and has the ongoing responsibilities and discipline to contend with.

Former relationships with married friends tend to slip away and a great deal of social isolation can be experienced by both the man and woman. Holidays and anniversaries with their emotional overtones are especially difficult periods for those suffering loss.

Healing measures

As with every crisis, it is important to keep in close touch with all your feelings and get them expressed in a safe place. This may mean giving conscious permission for your Criticizer or Abandoned Child to express themselves. One caution: you choose the time, place and person who hears. The temptation for some is simply to "splat" with everyone, everywhere.

Sharing with friends may help for a while. But if overused they ordinarily tend to pull away. For intense or continuing feelings, seek professional counseling from your rabbi, minister, priest or a marriage counselor.

Check your local community for self-help groups. Sharing with others going through a similar crisis is extremely helpful. It drastically cuts down on loneliness.

Above all, give yourself quality mourning time to deal with your loss—to weep, rehash, say goodbye. This holds true whether or not death is involved. The death of a relationship is as painful and in some cases even more so than the death of a person. The more you were attached to and dependent on the other the more strongly you will feel a hole for that which has been an important part of you.

Many universities, colleges, high school adult education departments, churches, synagogues and clinics have classes for those suffering such a loss. YMCAs have special groups for widowed, divorced and single parents to help you work through your situation. We Care, a self-help discussion group started in 1972, can be contacted.* If there is not a chapter in your community, they can perhaps help you start one. Check your phone directory for a listing of Parents Without Partners, and Momma.† They specialize in speakers, discussions and social activities.

Get meaningfully involved in work, projects, activities and hobbies of personal interest to you. The more inner turmoil you feel, ordinarily the more helpful it is to structure your time concretely. Allot specific time for handling the Critical or Abandoned Child feelings, some for Adult outward focus and some for being a kind Nurturer to You. Take a day at a time, as looking ahead too far gives your Frightened or Discouraged Child an opportunity to play havoc in your life.

The least helpful approach is to clam up, withdraw and wait for someone to rescue you, much as you might like to. Dedicate yourself to increasing your self-worth in all the ways suggested in this book. Nothing attracts others to you like your own self-confidence. Avoid giving one person (the departed one) or situation the power to define you.

Pay particular attention to positive health practices. A balanced diet, adequate rest and vigorous physical exercise help minimize the stress your body is going through.

Most who are divorced or widowed do remarry. It helps to see your present situation as a transition period. Seen this way, it can be a self-renewal time so that your future relationships are based on good feelings about yourself. The past can be used as a steppingstone to personal growth.

* We Care Foundation, 121 Broadway, No. 517, San Diego, CA 92101.
† For information about single mothering, write Momma, P. O. Box 5759, Santa Monica, CA 90404.

Middle-aged marriage

If you're in your forties or fifties, your marriage is particularly vulnerable to stress. It is during this period that the identity crisis of the middle years most often hits. Actually it can come anywhere between twenty and sixty—whenever you suddenly or gradually realize you won't live forever.

Middlescence brings a sharper awareness of time. Graying temples, wrinkles, glasses, thinning hair, thickening waistlines, reduced energy—each is concrete evidence that youth is slipping. You may find yourself seeking romantic flings or attachments particularly with someone younger than you. Your middle-aged mate is a daily reminder of where you are. Often it is not so much the new lover you're after as the reassurance that you have as much appeal as you had a quarter century ago. Your fling helps you deny your mortality.

The empty-nest syndrome, the menopause and perhaps the existence of grandchildren may remind women that youth is past. Much as you may enjoy the lessened responsibilities, much as you may love your grandchildren, the implications are clear. Men and many women may face the fact that their youthful dreams of power and success have gone unfulfilled. If not, they may have failed to bring the fantasied satisfactions.

This is a period of in-turning, of wondering and maybe fearing what the future holds. If you have aging parents it is a sharp reminder that your turn will come—and all too quickly.

You may suddenly stop in the midst of all your pressures and/or successes to wonder what it's all for. For some of you life may suddenly seem purposeless. All that striving, all that accumulating, all those pressures—what for?

And intermingled may come a vague or clear mourning for those closed chapters—the lost dreams, illusions and youthful ideals, the unfulfilled hopes, the past opportunities and meaningful periods that cannot be relived or recaptured. The mid-life lesson that our security does not lie in others is a hard pill for some to swallow.

With so much going on in each partner, it is easy to see why the middle-aged marriage is a fragile affair. It needs special nurturing. With heightened vulnerability and sensitivity we need to give and receive reassurance. And if self-worth is low or shaky, you need extra support.

Antidotes to middlescence

Once again, giving yourself permission to get in touch with all your feelings and expressing them through safe outlets is central.

Sharing with others who face similar pressures goes a long way toward accepting the inevitable. When husbands and wives with fifteen to thirty years of memories behind them openly and empathically share their inner experiencing, a new closeness comes.

If your mate does not choose that route, share with a friend or start a sharing group. It's amazing when one opens up how others gain courage to follow suit. There is no greater support than knowing you are not alone in your feelings. And if you have one safe spot in which you can openly share, the relationships where you cannot are less troublesome to accept.

Use your creative urges to see what and how you can simplify your life so that your energies are not scattered all over the map. Rather they are saved for those areas that bring the most joy. Activities that have special meaning for you are ones your Nurturing Parent would encourage.

Part of the mid-life crisis comes from unlived parts of you that clamor to be expressed. If you've been very active, the passive suddenly appeals. If you've been an achiever, not being achievement-oriented may feel good. If you've been uninvolved, participation often looks exciting. Regardless, what are some of the things you've always wanted to do but never taken time for? Tennis, swimming, pottery, jogging, painting, writing, traveling, singing, drifting, learning a foreign language, getting a college education or starting a new career or business? Now you have time.

To say you're too old to start is a copout. Thousands of fifties, sixties and beyond are proving the point. If you start piano playing at fifty you're not too likely to end up in Carnegie Hall. But why deny yourself the pleasure of learning to play for your own and possibly friends' enjoyment? It would be the Critical Parent Voice that says you have to demand perfection of yourself or that you're over the hump. Your Nurturing Parent would say, "Go to it and enjoy."

Concentrate on all the health practices that build you up. Let your Natural Child out all the way. You are never too old unless you think you are. Remember, your full potentials would take several lifetimes to develop. Where there's a will there's a way.

When you look at those in their eighties and nineties who have vigor and zest for life, you find people who have kept their minds and bodies active. The late Paul Bragge, a nonagenarian who jogged, swam, lectured, taught and wrote, said, "To rest is to rust." He wasn't talking about franticness but about not retiring from life.

If one door closes, look around for another to push open. As long as you are young in spirit you are ageless. And this agelessness splashes out to renew your relationships as well as yourself. It goes without saying, you become an inspiration for all.

The mid-life crisis can activate your Scared Child. If your mate is at the same stage, you then have two Scared Kids who may have trouble giving emotional support to one another. But awareness that you're both there together and open sharing can be the tie that binds.

Middlescence, even for the high self-esteemer, involves the search for a particular quality of life—a mellowing of many earlier strivings, a reassessment of values, priorities and goals, a questioning of future personal possibilities. There is less focus on merging or having the mate be a parent. And more on being a separate and distinct person in your own right.

Those who experience the Real Self move closer to the irreversible Inner Essence of their Beingness. Developing the Inner becomes an exciting process. The dawning of real wisdom can be the gift of the mid-years to those who affirm themselves. Growing older means growing wiser and more in touch with what it is possible to be in human Beingness terms.

The "ker-plunk" phenomenon

Early in marriage most couples have a forward thrust. They focus on jointly held tangible goals: setting up a home, establishing careers, perhaps starting a family and getting the children well on their way.

Those, however, who press relentlessly toward such goals often experience a "ker-plunk" when the major ones are reached. "Now what?" Goals and roles may lose their fizz—like stale Cokes.

If we look at those who avoid the "ker-plunk" or move past it, we invariably find people who are less goal-oriented than relationship-oriented. They are less focused on outer tangibles than interpersonal intangibles. They move toward what speaks to them but they take time to enjoy the process on the way.

They relish and let in the affection of others. They delight in giving affection. They enjoy co-operating and sharing and communicating. But their talk is noticeably free of "Ain't it awful" or "See how yukky I am." Problems are seen as interesting challenges. They know how to play. As one zestful ninety-year-old put it, "If I can do something about a situation, I do it; if I can't, I work around it. Life's too short to moan about what I cannot change. You miss all the fun that way."

If trying to arrive takes precedence over the process, look to your tapes. Give yourself permission to be less driven and "Think relationship."

Reaching out

Even as you get your own internal house in order, reach out. Recall Hillel's statement, "If you are not for you, who will be? If you are only for you, what's the purpose? If not now, when?"

As has been repeatedly pointed out in this book, it is easier to be affectionate, to care, share, get involved and co-operate when you have this same relationship with yourself. But to make sure you don't concentrate solely on yourself to the exclusion of others, keep daily track for a while of your reach-outs to others. Remember, they need affirmation just as you do. Tally one up for each genuine recognition stroke you give away. Try a minimum of two apiece daily for each family member and at least one daily for a non-family member. For starters, try a genuine smile;

an approving glance;

a warm embrace;

an *appreciative* thank you;

honest excitement for another's triumph;

a casserole for someone;

passing along a compliment about another;

sharing a funny story or joke;

a soft touch;

giving a family member a foot massage;

inviting an acquaintance to do something with you;

an appreciation note to your child's teacher, principal, group leader;

a similar note to your doctor or dentist or mailman;

helping another out with a chore;

a non-birthday cake;

a just-to-say-"hi" call;

a letter to a lonely one;

asking a stranger from your church/club for after-meeting coffee;

a love note on your mate's or child's pillow or by the dinner plate;

time for a leisurely visit;

a gentle tone;

a welcome call/note to a new neighbor;

a kind word to the manager of a store/restaurant for a clerk's service;

a "yard" flower by each dinner plate;

interested focus when another speaks;

a surprise shoeshine;

gentleness when someone's cross.

Let your creativity go wild. Everyone you live with, everyone you meet can use a little sunshine that comes especially from you.

Winners

A young child was looking at a photograph of a human ovum surrounded by thousands of sperm at its cell membrane. Her mother was explaining the picture to her. She concluded her explanation by saying, "Out of all those sperm only one will enter to join the egg. And those two cells will make the new baby."

The child asked, "Which sperm gets to do that?"

"Oh, I don't know," replied her mother. "Maybe the one that gets there first."

The youngster was quiet for a moment and then gleefully chirped, "Hey, that means we all start life as winners."

Out of the mouths of babes.

Yes, each of us begins life with the potential to win—to have high self-esteem . . . Wholeness . . . joy. To help our youngsters along that path it is crucial that we look to ourselves and our marriage. Parents who find nurturing joy in themselves and in each other are more likely to enjoy their children.

Continued clinging to old Critical tapes, refusal to grow free of your fears and dependencies, avoidance of developing your own strengths interfere with increasing self-worth, with enjoying marriage, sex and parenting. When you don't "need" from your mate you are freer to affirm and accept. Dependency and Critical tapes are not conducive to happiness in coupling or in facing your advancing years.

As we've seen, a Critical Self Belief System causes you and others untold pain. A Nurturing Belief System erases this. But the yeast that allows the bread of your self-worth to rise high lies in your ongoing connectedness with the true wonder of You. Let's see who You really are.

· FOURTEEN ·

WHO YOU TRULY ARE

From what was to what is

There is a remarkably unattractive insect whose gills force it to live in water for one to five years. Twelve or more times it sheds its skin; each time it remains waterbound.

Eventually it crawls from the muddy water to the top of a reed or up on a rock. At last after the final shedding what it is to be has come forth. Emerging with a long slender body and gauze-like, iridescent wings, it is the beautiful dragonfly. A whole new life-style is now possible. It breathes air, feels the sun's warmth and it flies!

This graceful flyer comes from the ugliest of bugs. Repeatedly it shuffles off the outer that is no longer appropriate. It then needs to pull *itself* out of the mud and water to new life. Unless it does, it cannot use the power within. Had it tried to cling to the old limitations, if it refused growth and change, if it had waited for someone else to free it, it would never have emerged to fulfill the promise of its birth.

Unless we *remove ourselves* from inappropriate past programmings that keep us mudbound and waterlogged—unless we lay claim to the creative Life Force within—we cannot fly free.

The final task

Now that you have redesigned your self-image—the packaged "Me"—you need to touch base with the Real Dweller within that package.

Your Nurturer, Adult and Natural Child serve as a gentle self-support system. They are servants, not masters. They form the Surface You with which to operate in the outer world. They provide a comfortable House for You to live in. They form the vehicle through which you express the Inner You. The Real You lives within the House of Self you build, but it is not the House.

The final task is to identify with—become one with—this Essential Inner Being.

You see You are more than a mere tape selector, stage director or self-esteem builder. These analogies have been used only to give you the tools for designing a comfortable House of Self—a positive self-image. Without this self-nurturing it is difficult if not impossible to connect with the Real You. But it is the sustained contact with who You truly are that ends your diligent search, that brings true tranquillity . . . peace. It is through this contact that Self healing takes place.

Back we go then to our original question: who is the Real You?

You know that dogs hear sounds outside your range of hearing. Microscopes and telescopes prove that even perfect human vision is limited to a particular range. When you look at a table or your hand, you see a solid mass of definite size and shape. Yet physics proves that what appears solid is in reality not solid at all. It is instead mostly empty space with the tiniest of particles spinning in particular patterns within that space.

Our senses, then, yours and mine, cannot "see" the Truth of what is. Our sense organs pick up only the most gross or dense slice of what seems to exist—the outer appearance. *We cannot rely on them alone to define ourselves.*

If you fill your tub, the water has the same smooth appearance throughout the tub. If you place a small mechanical swirler in one part of the tub, the water above it takes on a different pattern. If you pull the plug, the water above the drain forms a funneled pattern. If the water drained out over a pile of rocks yet another pattern would emerge. Regardless of the "look" of the water—level, swirling, funneling, rippling—it is made up of the same particles.

Just so, each of us is a unique constellation of identical Life Stuff. Your pattern or "assemblage," however, is like no other.

How unique are you?

Most of us give lip service to the uniqueness of each person. And then we lightly toss the fact aside. My hope is that when you learn just *how* unique you are you will never again cavalierly dismiss this knowing.

The DNA molecule determines your inherited qualities. Mathematicians estimate that the DNA molecule can theoretically unite in $10^{2,400,000,000}$ ways. By comparison they estimate that the entire universe contains only 10^{76} atomic particles.* This means that to find two people genetically strung together alike you'd need $10^{2,400,000,000}$ people.

Mind-boggling!

To grasp the enormity of this number, realize what you would need simply to write out this figure. If each zero were one inch wide, you would need a strip of paper 37,000 miles long!

If you translated this figure into units its enormity becomes even more staggering. Robert Jastrow, one of our leading astronomers, estimates the size of our universe as ten billion light-years.† There are six trillion miles in one light-year. If you took dots one millimeter in diameter and laid them end to end *from our earth to the end of our universe and back* you would have to do that $10^{399,999,977}$ times to equal $10^{2,400,000,000}$!‡

Now do you realize how rare you are?

The likelihood of another genetically put together into your unique pattern at any time in the past, anywhere today or any time in the future is so infinitesimally small as to be inconceivable. And

* David Bergamini and Editors of *Life*, *Mathematics*. New York: Time Inc., 1963, p. 147.
† Robert Jastrow, *Red Giants and White Dwarfs*. New York: Harper & Row, 1967, p. 13.
‡ I am indebted to Dr. Robert A. Smith, Professor of Statistics and Computer Design, Chairman of Department of Educational Psychology, University of Southern California, for this calculation.

this uniqueness is quite apart from all the conditioning that has been reacted to by this uniqueness of yours.

To say that you are a special event in the universe is not Pollyanna drivel. It is a fact of life.

How irrelevant to compare yourself to another! How totally impossible to try to be a carbon copy!

**Our universe apparently
does not indulge in
duplicates.**

Each creation is virtually unrepeatable.

Do you know who You truly are?

You are an unprecedented event in the universe!

You are not a world premiere; you are a universal one!

You are an expression of the Source.

No person, thing or event can erase this truth.

Stop and concretely experience the magnitude of this fact. Let it sink deep into your bones and tissues. Feel its impact.

This awareness doesn't mean you look at others with disdain, for you realize they too are as rare as You. A lasting and responsible value system falls more easily into place when you are in touch with the wonder of You and the wonder of others. If I see the negatives in you, I see the outer, the behavior, the appearance. I see what separates us.

If I see the True You, I see the Inner. I see what unites us.

Do you want to see a miracle? All you have to do is look in the mirror! All you have to do is look around you! Each of us is made of the same Life Stuff. Yet each of us is in essence without peer.

The great paradox

We all know that both within our bodies and without there is constant change. Change is woven into the very fabric of life.

Yet the great paradox is that at the center of the cacophony of change there is *changelessness*. Energy dances into new patterns and forms but energy itself is changeless.

The Real You represents a separate entity in the vastness of Creation. *New but related beyond time and space to all others . . .* to all Creation.

Within the pattern that makes you up, there is a non-physical Be-ingness—a Conscious-Awareness, a Life Force, an Inner Power, a Spirit. Choose the word you can embrace. *The Real You is that Be-ingness, that Conscious-Awareness, that Inner Power.* It is more than your body, mind, emotions or self-image. But most of us at best experience only a small and limited portion of it, if at all. When your self-picture embraces and becomes one with this inde-scribable Fountainhead, you experience Wholeness.

Your awareness can expand to become more fully conscious of your Core. A great miracle happens once you connect with the Inner Essence of your Being—with your Essential Life Stuff.

There you find the infinite peace of Love.

Love is an energy, a cohesive force that keeps us together. An absence of love causes pain and deterioration. Love is a healing force that unites you to all Life. Connecting with the Uncondi-tioned Real You permits you to see yourself *with* the eyes of Love.

You are more than you think you are. If you measure yourself by the standards of humankind you fall short here and there. But when you experience yourself by Love's standards—by the sheer miracle in your Existence—and your relatedness to all Creation—then you touch your true glory.

Remember, you can be fooled by outer, material appearances. But the Real You is apart from them. Connecting with the Source within releases a great new power . . . the power of Love.

Whom do you most need to love you? *You. If a thousand others love you and you love yourself not, others' love will never be enough.*

Who is the greatest withholder of your love? Your negative tapes . . . your seeing yourself through the limited vision of others who had not captured their own glory. Only you can release that dis-torted vision. Once you do, you no longer see yourself as a lone and solitary being. You "see" beyond your sight.

As you capture the flavor of the awesome and miraculous Essence of You, you experience an At-Onement-with-all-life. You have a bone and muscle knowing of relatedness to the Family of Human-kind and beyond that to the Universal. All Life is reperceived. In Love we become whole. Experiencing this Truth sets you free.

The Real You does not live *for* the moment, but flows *in* the nowness of the Cosmic. The Real You—the Big "I" that is part of the Eternal Creative Force—needs to be central in your awareness.

Repositioning your base

By shifting to an ongoing sense of who You truly are, you reposition yourself. Your base of operations is now from the inside out, not from the outside in.

It cannot be overemphasized that being grounded in the quiet consciousness of the formless, unlimited changelessness of your Essential Center lets you see yourself, others and the world from an entirely different vantage point.

As Ken Keyes, Jr. has said, "A loving person lives in a loving world. A hostile person lives in a hostile world. Everyone you meet is your mirror."*

Centering in calm gives a new perspective on outside pressures. It is much like standing in a cozy room watching the varying elements of an outside storm. You are safe from the vicissitudes of the outer.

Centeredness does not mean you are withdrawn from or uninvolved with the outer. But you are less buffeted about. Those who survive impossible pressures are invariably committed to, grounded in and identified with a larger Whole.

Trying to communicate what you experience by centering in your Beingness is like trying to describe what a strawberry tastes like. You have to taste the fruit before you can know.

If you only read these words, you forfeit the experience. If you actively and consistently practice centering you come to the Truth of You.

Centering

You may already have a centering plan. The particular techniques you follow may already give you the tapping-into-the-Source experience discussed here. If so, you know that only by diligently setting aside this daily renewal time do you reap the benefits. The

* Ken Keyes, Jr., *Handbook to Higher Consciousness.* Berkeley: Living Love Center, 1974, pp. 43, 44.

shakier your self-worth the more frequently you need centering time.

Tapping your Core Self requires turning within. But rippled ponds don't allow us to peer into the depths. Your mind racing with needs and concerns screens your Beingness from your experience. If you do not have a centering plan, try the following.

The first requirement is to still the body; the second is to still the mind; the third requires definite action.

Sit comfortably in a quiet spot. Early morning and late afternoon are often preferred times; regardless, avoid centering when you have just eaten a big meal or done strenuous physical exercise.

Gently close your eyes after reading these instructions. Starting with your feet, ever so slowly tense the muscles, hold them tight for a moment and gradually relax them. Repeat this slow tensing and relaxing with each muscle group in your body (calves, knees, thighs, buttocks, abdomen, chest, shoulders, arms, hands, neck, face). Now slowly tense your whole body and gently let it relax. Check your body to see if any area seems tight. If so, softly send it a message to let go. Give your body permission to be completely quiet.

To still your mind, focus all your attention on your breathing; feel your lungs gently expand and contract. Focus on the feel of the air in your nostrils as it comes in and goes out . . . in and out . . . in and out. (You may prefer to focus on special music or a single word, repeated as if at the center of your Being. A word such as "God," "Peace," "One," "Love," "Harmony," "Release" or any word that holds special personal meaning.)

Now envision a soft, warm light flooding you—moving ever so gradually from the top of your head to the bottom of your feet. Trace its warm glow slowly as it infuses each body part. Be very still. Quietly tune in to the *feel* of the soft, warm light. Quietly and receptively listen. Do this now, relaxing as described, focusing, feeling the soft warm light filling you.

Stilling the body and mind at regular periodic intervals has a marvelously quieting effect. Daily stresses seem far less abrasive.

But the third step, which involves positive mental action, brings such benefits that I hope you do not stop with these first two steps.

It is *knowing* that is the crucial *active* step.

Positive mental action

A series of positive affirmations† is given below.

Each of the following affirmations needs to be done with closed eyes and centeredness. Open your eyes only long enough to read the next one and then close them while you focus on the one just read.

It will not be enough to mouth or simply think these words. You actively need to feel the truth of them. Vividly picture yourself as *being at one* with the particular statement. Pause after each sentence. *Take time* to become one with its meaning. Let that meaning completely penetrate your awareness. Do not move ahead to the next affirmation until you have consciously *fused* with this Truth about you. Each affirmation needs to become a personal *realization* for you.

Picture yourself about five feet out in front of you. Say to yourself,‡

I let go of all negative parts of the old "Me" package I put together.

I am unchained. I stand free.

I am a distinct addition to life.

I let no person, no event define or diminish the Real Me.

I embrace . . . I validate . . . I quietly inwardly celebrate the wonder of my Being.

My True Self is perfection in motion. It always has been; it always will be.

I am one with all Life.

Be still. Bathe in the Truth of You. Your Knower lives within. Your Knower is One with Universal Wisdom. You now refuse to imprison your splendor by playing puppet to past conditioning. You know who You are—a representative of Creation.

† A more extended list is included in the Checklist of Basic Ideas at the back of the book.
‡ A cassette ("WHO YOU TRULY ARE") with my personally taking you through relaxation and affirmation is available. For price write Creative Communications, Inc., P. O. Box 7780, Waco, Texas 76714-7780.

Remember, whatever you put after "I am" affects your self-worth, your consciousness, your outlook and your behavior. Whatever you consciously or subconsciously put after "I am," becomes a construction block in your House of Self. Whatever you associate yourself with through your "I am's" you claim. Identifying with that quality ("inferior," "inwardly free," etc.) builds that very trait into your "Me" package—your consciousness of You.

As you've no doubt experienced, others may try to hand you negative building blocks, but you can refuse to use them.

It is crucial to speak the Truth to yourself. Make a commitment not to bear false witness against your Self. If you find yourself "unable" to make these Self-affirming statements, the barrier will doubtlessly be your Criticizer's edict for Self negation. Choose to set it aside.

Positive pictures

In Chapter Eight we talked about "believing you can" as one way to activate your Nurturing Voice. This positive picturing is especially productive when you do it at the end of your centering-affirmation time.

Having affirmed your Core makes it easier to picture yourself possessing the positive qualities you seek. It truly is done unto you as you believe. It is necessary, therefore, to spend at least ten minutes vividly seeing yourself with the eyes of positive faith.

If you want the quality of warmth, picture yourself vividly as having that quality. As if on a movie screen—with your eyes closed —see yourself talking and relating to others warmly. Do this with any characteristic you want for yourself whether it is vibrant energy, quiet calm, gentleness, self-confidence, initiative, courage, freedom from fear or whatever.

Any characteristic you want only lies in sleeping potential within. Seeing yourself in possession of it awakens this trait. Work with only one, at most two, qualities at a time.

The final, essential step as you slowly emerge from centering and picturing is to do so with the *conviction* that the quality you have identified with and visualized is now yours. And then act as if it is.

Take the *experiencing* of the basic affirmations and the positive mental pictures *with you* into everyday living. Let them form the basis from which you act, much like a kind of "psychological background music" as you go about your daily activities.

Sound strange? All I'm suggesting is that you become aware of what you are already doing. And if your self-esteem is low or shaky, you may be sure your "background music" is a dirge or at best downbeat. What you will now be doing is putting on an upbeat song—the Song of Life. In no time with picturing, conviction and practice this way of experiencing yourself will become a way of life.

It is extremely helpful to keep a daily log and note each evening what you experienced both within yourself and from others.

Centered in Wonder, Love and a positive self-image you see all life through the window of affirmation. Then you are grounded in peace.

**To continue the outer search
is to avoid a
decision for and commitment to
the inner.**

We each have that freedom. But we're more honest with ourselves when we freely admit, "I do not choose to give up looking for validation from other people out there. I do not choose to connect with my Center and through it to the Universal."

The rainbows of materialism, power, status and distractions do not bring the gold of peace, love and contentment. When you identify with the "Me" you put together from the limited vision of others, you disconnect from the Real You. Only through tapping the Source Within can you experience who You truly are. Only then can you fully celebrate others.

Your purpose

Does it make a difference that you exist? Of course it does. No one is your duplicate; your gifts are solely yours. Large or small, there is some contribution that only you can make.

Everywhere there is a need for what you have to offer. Quiet Self celebration brings a serenity that allows you to contribute to the world and those around you in your own never reoccurring ways. Your purpose is to unfold your Special Beingness. There is no question about it. Experiencing your self-worth is the key to your life. It is contagious to all around you.

Dis-cover means to take off the cover. Self-discovery means lifting the cover of masks, lifting the layer of an inappropriate Belief System to experience the Real You.

You are one of a kind.

Your permanent home

You know that when you are "in love" you feel beautiful. And the whole world looks beautiful.

The point is that you are always *in Love*.

Distress comes when you are unaware of this fact. It comes when you separate from this knowing. The Eternal is both without and within.

Peace and Love lie at your Center. Peace and Love are already yours. You have only to claim them.

What you have been seeking, you already have.

**Serenity is a gift
from You
to you.**

Welcome to Wholeness ... to Inner Liberation.
Welcome to the joy and power of being You.
Welcome Home!

For an inspiring treasure house of wisdom and insights-to-live-with, refer to EMBRACING LIFE by Dorothy Corkille Briggs (Doubleday, 1985). This book focuses on handling the issues of love, loss, change and relationships victoriously.

CHECKLIST OF BASIC IDEAS

Here are the kernel ideas we've talked about. They can serve as booster shots along the path of daily Self nurturing.

What's Here for You

1. The key to inner peace lies in Self affirmation. This is not conceit but a quiet celebration that you are You.
2. You cannot always change the outer or others. But you can change your reactions. You and you alone write your own ticket to serenity.
3. The path to inner peace requires awareness, courage, decision and action.

Your Belief System About You

1. Who are you? You are not your name, age, size, shape, roles, values, relationships or self-image. You are your Essential

Being, unlike any other. You are changeless yet always in process.

2. Your self-image—the package you call "Me"—was put together by you from how others saw and treated you. It may or may not be accurate. Regardless, it forms your personal Belief System about you.

3. Negative past experiences and teachings that made you feel unlovable and inadequate cause you to behave accordingly. Negative self-statements limit the options you give yourself. They imprison you.

4. Your self-image is learned. You can reprogram defective self-attitudes so that you live with a strong sense of personal self-worth.

5. A self-image of inadequacy becomes increasingly negative with age unless its existence is challenged and reworked.

6. Winners are inwardly free of destructive programming. Losers base their lives on the false belief that they are unlovable.

How You Got Where You Are Today

1. Your mind is like a multi-decked tape recorder with several "I's" or personality parts from which you can speak.

2. The "felt" Voice comes from the Child-in-you. The "thought" Voice comes from the Adult-in-you. The "taught" Voice comes from the Parent-in-you.

3. The amount of Not-OKness you feel is directly proportional to the size and strength of your Critical Parent tape. You have come to see yourself through the eyes of significant others from your past.

4. Your "Unacceptable Me" is the basis of low self-esteem.

5. The talk and treatment of others becomes your own self-talk and self-treatment; it is either for or against you.

6. High self-esteemers have little negative self-talk; they are Nurturing Parents to themselves. They are able to play, enjoy and express, but they stay in contact with reality and are responsible to themselves and others.

The Power of Not-OKness

1. Your Inner Child believes the psychological climate it grew up in is the only kind worth having. The Sad/Bad/Mad Child-in-you will strenuously resist changing the "Me" you have built. It seeks the comfort of the known; it is fearful of closeness to others (the source of past pain), and it resists giving up dependency.

2. Your Not-OK Child is kept alive today when you parent yourself with the same talk and attitudes of past others.

3. To increase your self-worth you do not need to change your Self. You need to change your self-talk and your negative beliefs about your Self. You can choose to become your own Nurturing Parent.

4. In your internal cast of characters the troublemakers will be your Not-OK Child and your Critical Parent tapes. They are hooked into the love of power. They try to manipulate, control and win. Your Nurturer, Adult and Natural Child are concerned with the power of love. They are the ones that work for your best interests.

5. You can choose to redesign the package you call "Me." No one can ever take the power of choice away from you. Only you can give it away.

Watch Your Language

1. The path to inner personal freedom involves scrupulously zeroing in on how you make pain for yourself. Continually ask yourself, "What kind of parent am I to me?"

2. Your Critical Voice can be recognized by its use of such words as "should," "must," "ought," "have to." They set up a master-slave dialogue within.

3. Change these words to those of the self-responsible Adult and the Nurturing Parent: "wish," "prefer," "want," "choose," "feel," "desire."

4. Change every "can't" (Helpless Child Voice) to a "won't" or "choose not to" except those that truly come from a physical inability. Own up to the responsibility of your choices. Winners don't play Helpless; rather they claim their choices as their own.

5. You can choose not to react to others. You do this by giving them the space to do their number while refusing to take their bait.

6. Symptoms have payoffs. They keep us from certain feelings or acts one part of us does not want to deal with. They often bring secondary gains. You free yourself by going after what you want directly.

Expectations That Cause Pain

1. Reasonable expectations are nurturing; unreasonable ones cause pain.

2. Your Inner Criticizer will ask for perfection in feelings, thoughts and deeds. Give yourself permission to be less than perfect. Do not cling to past mistakes, rather release them.

3. Seeking everyone's approval means giving up your own Self.

4. You are not alone in your feelings of inadequacy or insecurity.

5. Self-expectations need to be realistic, not impossible.

6. When you are upset, check to see what expectation has gone unmet.

7. Demand/need expectations born of "This is due me" cause trouble. They come from the Child or Critical Voice.

8. Avoid playing Dependent Child by changing what once may have been appropriately dire needs to wishes or preferences. Ask yourself what's the worst that could happen if they go unmet.

Other Painful Expectations

1. Nurture yourself by concentrating on what's right about you rather than what's wrong. Consistently give yourself private "support-talk." Relish your strengths and successes.

2. Give up the beliefs that things "should" always go as you want them to; that others "should" match your feelings, attitudes and values; that you need to compare yourself to others; that life and others will always be fair; that smooth sailing is the norm; that others "should" know how you feel or what you want without being told.

3. When you overreact, know that an earlier pain experienced as a threat to your Inner Child's survival is probably being triggered. Unexpressed feelings from that first pain need to be expressed through acceptable outlets in a safe place. Preferably to an empathic, supportive person.

4. You defuse the tender spots by allowing the Child or Critical Voice to express its feelings, by nurturing your own Inner Child and then giving your Adult a job that allows an outer focus.

5. Dealing with past hurts and hidden painful expectations rather than burying them is part of Self nurturing.

6. If emotional conflicts or symptoms are serious or incapacitating do not try to treat yourself. You are a Nurturing Parent to yourself when you seek competent help.

Judgment: the Dance of Death

1. "Shoulds" cause expectations that lead to judgments. Self-blame is at the core of all emotional disorder.

2. To avoid Self judgment react to your behavior, feelings and attitudes.

3. See your person as separate from your behavior, thoughts and feelings; otherwise your Self worth is lowered with each misstep.

4. Remember all new learning takes place in stages. You will become aware of reverting to old tapes *after* you've used them. Then you will be aware *during* the time you use old solutions. The final stage will eventually come; you will remember to use the new step *before* you revert to the old. Turn on your Nur-

turer and be patient with yourself; be supportive as you move
to change old ways.

5. Translate the judgment of others into their reactions toward
your behavior. Avoid letting outside judgments become Self
judgments.

Copied or Free

1. Many of your attitudes, reactions and behaviors are copied
from early models. You Self nurture when you weed out any
anti-life injunctions.

2. Check that you are not playing Total Opposite, for you are as
unfree on that tape as when you play Total Mimic.

3. Seek prolonged exposure to pro-life models for those positive
qualities you want to encourage. Let your natural inclination
to imitate be directed toward copying nurturing permissions.

4. Give yourself permission to let all feelings into your awareness
without judgment. You disown a vital part of your person if
you deny any feeling. Do not act on those that are irresponsible to yourself or others.

Role or Real

1. Give yourself permission to stop pretending, masking, role-
playing. Remember you are a person above and beyond all the
relationships you are involved with. Give yourself permission
to be appropriately real. This involves risk-taking but the
affirmation you get will be for what is rather than for a phony
front.

2. Past roles you may have adopted were simply brave survival
responses. Do not judge them; rather challenge their present
usefulness.

3. Giving up your masks and your fear of rejection means you
give yourself the freedom to be You.

4. When you are freely yourself you welcome your opposites; you
do not ask yourself to have only one set of emotions. You ac-

cept that you will experience the full range of feelings. You refuse to let others put you into either-or boxes.

A Friend for You

1. Do you treat yourself as gently as you would a precious friend? If not, why not?

2. Are you being friendly to your body by giving it nutritious food, adequate sleep, exercise and physical checkups? If not, why not?

3. Do you let the Natural Child in you play for the pure fun and enjoyment of the activity without the pressure to compete, achieve or produce? If not, why not?

4. Practice staying in touch with all of your senses to savor the flavor of each moment in time.

5. Take time to indulge your creativity, curiosity and spontaneity. Give yourself permission to venture into the new.

6. Give yourself periodic gifts (some cost nothing) that are gentle kindnesses to you.

7. Avoid wallowing in the "if only's" of the past and the "what if's" of the future. Focus on the present—it's the only time you really have.

8. Believing you can, having faith in You and your abilities in spite of setbacks is part of Self nurturing.

9. Cultivate many friends; each one has a special gift for you—a piece of their uniqueness to share.

Making Coupleships Work

1. Seeing others through the eyes of blame or pain stands in the way of constructive coupling.

2. Loving another because he or she rounds you out puts you in a needing, dependent and ultimately resentful position. It keeps you from being whole in your own right.

3. Too often we choose partners and friends like the family member who failed to validate our lovability.

4. Parent-child, master-slave couplings are fraught with continual dominance-submission power struggles and efforts to shape the other up.

5. When either partner pushes to change the relationship the original basis for coming together is threatened. Much static results. But such a movement is a great opportunity for both to grow free and move to co-equal relating.

6. Adults with strong unmet dependency needs have trouble parenting. Their own need to lean is threatened by their children's need to be dependent on them.

7. Many forces are at work to weaken the institution of marriage and family. The answer is not divorce or an affair since you take your taping with you in all relationships. The answer rather lies in giving up destructive tapes by becoming your own Nurturing Parent, by becoming whole in your own right.

8. You and your partner both have the potential to grow whole. This means releasing the other and relentlessly working on your own case. This calls for an ongoing self-inventory, open communication, commitment and risking closeness. Enriching relationships come with caring, awareness, honesty, commitment, patience and effort.

Issues in Coupling

1. Critical Parent injunctions against body pleasuring need to be set aside if sex is to be enjoyed.

2. Commitment is based on mutual freedom to trust, mutual willingness to know and be known and mutual emotional support.

3. If you have experienced a broken love relationship through death, divorce or separation the lost attachment to the person and role triggers off feelings of denial, abandonment, anger, grief, divided loyalties and social isolation.

4. Quality mourning time, sharing with professional helpers or others who have suffered similarly, meaningful involvements and taking a day at a time all help you through the transition

period. Avoid withdrawing or trying to skip over the grief process.

5. Middlescence is a special time for re-evaluating your self-image, values and life goals. Denying your mortality only puts off the eventual task of facing it.

6. Open sharing of feelings, keeping active mentally and physically and giving your undeveloped potentials permission to be expressed can bring heightened joys to your advancing years. Take time to enjoy and reach out.

Who You Truly Are

1. Our senses pick up only the most dense slice of what seems to be. Outer appearances do not reveal the whole Truth of your Being.

2. The likelihood of another being genetically like you is $10^{2,400,000,000}$ power!

3. Our universe does not indulge in duplicates; therefore, it is totally irrelevant to compare your uniqueness with that of any other.

4. Although we are all made of the same Life Stuff, the Real You is a separate entity in the universe.

5. Within the assemblage making you up is a non-physical Be-ingness, a Conscious Awareness, an Inner Power centered in Love.

6. Tapping into the miracle of your Existence through centering, affirmation and positive picturing repositions you in peace. What you have to offer can never be duplicated. You, like everyone else, are without peer. Remember, your inner serenity is your gift to You. You return home to the House of Love when you maintain an ongoing connectedness with the Real You.

Basic affirmations with visualization possibilities (Choose those you like or make up your own.)

I let go of all negative parts of the old "Me" package I put together.

(Imagine your skin as a delicate parchment. See it begin to crack and peel off against the pressure of the Inner Growing You. Like the dragonfly, experience yourself as wriggling free of the bondage of the old "Me" casing. Experience an inner movement expanding your person as it breaks loose of the old "skin." Know you can never fit into that old package again.)

I am unchained . . . I stand free.
(See yourself as standing tall and sure and free. See the old "skin" you have shed lying in bits and pieces around your feet. It served its purpose once; see it as totally useless now.)

I let my total Being absorb these Truths.
(Imagine these Truths flowing in through your nose and ears and pores, sinking deep into your muscles and bones and organs.)

I am an unrepeatable miracle.
(See the endless stream of humankind from the beginning of time passing before you. Include the passing of the millions on earth today. Imagine the flow of all future generations passing by. Soak up the impact of this personal message—that none is like you. *Feel* it soaking in.)

I am a universal premiere . . . a distinct addition to life.
(Imagine seeing a great work of art unveiled for the first time. Freshly capture the vastness of your "firstness.")

My job is not to mimic . . . mine is to BE . . . to unfold the talents uniquely mine.
(Picture your Inner Splendor as a gradually unfolding bud. Stay with this image and watch the beauty and wonder of the unfoldment.)

I let no person, no event define or diminish the Real Me.
(Actively see outer arrows as sliding past you. They glance off; they do not touch your Person at all. No other can compress the incompressible You.)

I join hands with my Core Self.
(Clasp your hands in gentle friendship.)

I choose to be a loving friend to me.
(Imagine lovingly embracing your Essential Center.)

I embrace . . . I validate . . . I quietly inwardly celebrate the wonder of my Being.
   (Vividly picture your Real Self as a priceless jewel that you look at with awe.)

Each time I look in the mirror, I will see behind my eyes.
   (Imagine looking through to make contact with your deepest Center.)

I see my own miracle.
   (Experience contacting your Center Core of Love.)

I see with delight . . . the Inner Light.
   (Actively see a soft, warm glow in and around your Being.)

My True Core is perfection in motion. It always has been; it always will be.
   (Visualize the Inner Perfection created in You.)

I am whole. I am complete.
   (Feel the Life Beat in You. Get the feel of Wholeness, Completeness.)

I am related to all Creation. I am part of the great Whole.
   (See the inner glow—the Life Stuff—in You flowing out to meld with the Life Stuff of those near you, going beyond to meld with the Essence of all Creation.)

I am one with all Life.
   (See the Life Force like a delicate web uniting all. Feel, experience your connectedness. Stay with it. Know it is always there.)

I am still. I am completely still. I bathe in the Truth within.
   (See yourself as totally absorbing this Truth just as your total body absorbs the oxygen you breathe.)

I know who I am. I am a representative of Creation.
   (Picture yourself as being convinced of these affirmations. Know these statements are the Truth about You. Experience them as *realities* about You. Know that nothing can erase or dim these Truths.)

And so it is.
   (Quietly come out of your centering as you experience the inner glow of absolute conviction.)

READING GUIDE

Here are some books to serve as additional springboards to self-knowledge. This list is by no means exhaustive. But in simple terms each book looks at different angles of personal growth. Each new idea, each old one that is reinforced can add to your repertoire of Self-nurturing attitudes.

Bach, Richard. *Jonathan Livingston Seagull*. New York: Macmillan, 1970.

Branden, Nathaniel. *The Disowned Self*. Los Angeles: Nash, 1971.

Briggs, Dorothy Corkille. *Your Child's Self-Esteem*. New York: Doubleday, 1970.

Calden, George. *I Count—You Count*. Niles, Ill.: Argus, 1976.

Cole, Jim. *The Controllers*. Fort Collins, Colo.: Shields Pub. Co., Inc., 1971.

———. *The Facade*. Fort Collins, Colo.: Shields Pub. Co., Inc., 1970.

Daniels, Victor, and Laurence Horowitz. *Being and Caring*. San Francisco: San Francisco Book Co., Inc., 1976.

Glasser, William, M.D. *Positive Addictions*. New York: Harper & Row, 1976.

Greenwald, Jerry. *Be the Person You Were Meant to Be*. New York: Simon & Schuster, 1973.

Harris, Sidney J. *Winners and Losers*. Niles, Ill.: Argus, 1973.

James, Muriel, and Dorothy Jongeward. *Born to Win*. Reading, Mass.: Addison-Wesley Pub. Co., 1971.

Kirsten, Grace, and Richard Robertiello, M.D. *Big You Little You*. New York: Dial Press, 1977.

Krantzler, Mel. *Creative Divorce*. New York: M. Evans, 1971.

Lazarus, Arnold, and Allan Fay, M.D. *I Can If I Want To*. New York: William Morrow and Co., 1975.

Missildine, W. Hugh, M.D. *Your Inner Child of the Past*. New York: Simon & Schuster, 1963.

———. *Your Inner Conflicts: How to Solve Them*. New York: Simon & Schuster, 1975.

Newman, Mildred, and Bernard Berkowitz, with Jean Owen. *How to Be Your Own Best Friend*. New York: Random House, 1971.

Pietsch, William. *Human BE-ing*. New York: Lawrence Hill & Co., 1974.

Powell, John. *Fully Human, Fully Alive*. Niles, Ill.: Argus, 1976.

———. *The Secret of Staying in Love*. Niles, Ill.: Argus, 1974.

———. *Why Am I Afraid to Love?* Niles, Ill.: Argus, 1972.

———. *Why Am I Afraid to Tell You Who I Am?* Niles, Ill.: Argus, 1969.

Progoff, Ira. *At a Journal Workshop*. New York: Dialogue House Library, 1975.

Rubin, Theodore Isaac, M.D. *The Angry Book*. New York: Collier-Macmillan, 1969.

Satir, Virginia. *Peoplemaking*. Palo Alto, Ca.: Science & Behavior Books, Inc., 1972.

Sheehy, Gail. *Passages*. New York: Dutton, 1976.

Shostrum, Everett, and James Kavenaugh. *Between Man and Woman*. Los Angeles: Nash, 1971.

Smith, Manuel J. *When I Say No, I Feel Guilty*. New York: Bantam Books, 1975.

Stevens, John O. *Awareness: Exploring, Experimenting, Experiencing.* Moab, Utah: Real People Press, 1971.

Tanner, Ira J. *Loneliness: The Fear of Love.* New York: Harper & Row, 1973. Perennial Library edition, 1974.

For cassettes, pamphlets and study guides on increasing your self-esteem, write:

The Barksdale Foundation for the Furtherance
of Human Understanding,
P. O. Box 187
Idyllwild, CA 92349.

They hold periodic workshops and give information about starting home study groups.

The Catholic and Lutheran Churches and Jewish Synagogues in many parts of the country have Marriage Encounter Weekends that many couples have found extremely valuable in opening up communication lines between partners. If you are interested, check in your local community for such an offering. There are other religious denominations that are considering this program. You and your mate need not be a member of the denomination to participate.

INDEX